Run Church Run! is a clarion call to all leaders and believers that enhances our understanding of God's provision and intention for His Church at this urgent hour.

AYO DON-DAWODU
OASIS INT. CHURCH, UK

This is not a book that can be shunted into a sectional cul-de-sac. By being able to say that a book is from the *Word of Faith* camp or from the *Apostolic/Prophetic* camp or from the *Evangelical camp* we have ignored several sublime messages that God has sent to us.

But this is an inclusive book. It is wholistic without in any way compromising or losing its edge. It plots a thread through the history and within the context of the revelation - story and gives us insight into all that God has done, is doing, will do and how they all cohere to the grand revelation in the Eschaton.

I commend it highly also because though presenting a message of depth, it has been done so without undue verbosity and uncalled-for complexity.

Tokunbo is a golden voice to which we must all pay attention or pay the dire price of being sidelined.

ODE EYEOYIBO
EPIGNOSIA MINISTRIES, UK

Run Church Run! is an impassioned plea to the body of Christ to return to the basics of loving Jesus and reaching the world for Him. It is a call for unity that the "sons of God" may be revealed and that the world may see Jesus in and through His body. Reading *Run Church Run!* made me shout "Hallelujah!" This book not only shows us the way forward but tells us how to go about it. Read *Run Church Run!* It will stir you to do exploits for the King.

KATE JINADU
NEW COVENANT CHURCH, UK

Tokunbo Emmanuel is one of the leaders of God's 'Third-Day' army - the fruit of the gospel that went out from the islands and lands of Europe. The message of his new book is urgent and vital for today.

The Western church is in transition and the exceptional help that the Lord is sending represents a window of grace and opportunity that will not be open for long. It is imperative that the church goes forward armed with the authority and weaponry that God has promised for this time. We are faced by the opportunity of a full on revival which will complete the reformation and win back our continent, or the real possibility of a new dark ages that will eclipse even the remaining fires of kingdom life which currently give us hope.

So read this book and *Run Church Run!*

ROGER MITCHELL
PASSION, UK

This book comes with a warning for those who have no desire to hear Gods voice challenging them to fulfil their destiny. Every word from God is packed with life (*zoe*), vision and purpose. No word is wasted or frivolous. He is never 'trying to say' anything! He either speaks or is silent. He means what He says and says what He means.

Run Church Run! is a compelling wake up call for a Church at ease, with personal practical examples of God's dealing in a present day setting. God's words call the future into the present giving His Church a reason to stay covered and on course. This prophetic act is the single greatest hope of the 21st Century Church for where there is no vision the people perish or as another translation puts it the people 'is made naked'. This prophetic book is intended to cover the nakedness of the Church and enable us without shame to fulfil God's set mandate for His end time Church.

Run Church Run! will propel a response which we must not ignore. Tokunbo Emmanuel has heard yet again from God…Let him who has ears hear!

NIMS OBUNGE
FREEDOMS ARK, UK

Run Church Run! is a wake up call for the church of the Living God to arise to its purpose with urgency. There is an assignment to fulfil and the church can't afford to run oblivious to its responsibilities for the salvation of mankind. Christian's need to have a paradigm shift if the church of Christ is to embrace God's mandate.

In a fluid but precise style, Tokunbo Emmanuel calls on the body of Christ to position herself strategically and run the race set before her with purpose and exactitude. Every believer should find this book inspiring and instructional; a helpful guide to both the individual and the collective church body.

DR. ALBERT ODULELE
GLORY HOUSE, UK

In Pursuit of the Consummation of God's Eternal Purpose

RUN CHURCH RUN!

In Pursuit of the Consummation of God's Eternal Purpose

Tokunbo Emmanuel

MEGA! BOOKS
London, United Kingdom

CONTENTS

PART III: THE URGENCY OF THE HOUR:

Receive divine impetus for optimum speed on the tracks of global outreach through the force of divine revelation and the power of divine partnership.

APPENDICES:

To my darling wife, Linda,
my wonderful daughter, Destiny,
and my lovely son, Daniel.

*****

To Chimezie Onyebilanma,
Lola Amori.
and
the remaining "forty-something"
who attended,
and hopefully were impacted by,
Holiday Outreach 1991

*****

To the rising generation of people
who are committed to finishing
the purposes of God before the
coming of our Lord and King, Jesus Christ
(or before they sleep - whichever comes first).

ACKNOWLEDGEMENTS

Ever since the Lord gave me the title for this book more than ten years ago, my paths have crossed many important people. Space will not permit a detailed mention of each person's relevance in my life and to the writing of *Run Church Run!*

I am indebted to all the participants of *Holiday Outreach '91 & '92*. It was after these programmes that I received a clear mandate from God to write this book.

Special thanks to Rev. Emmanuel Aladiran for his helpful suggestions; Rev. Frank Ofosu-Appiah for encouraging me after reading the 1997 draft; my pastor; Rev. Kate Jinadu for her encouragement too; Rev. Hugh Osgood, for his wisdom and fatherly guidance; a number of ministers who read the script and gave positive feedback.

A big "thank you" to Dayo Fasina for her professional touch in proof-reading the typescript. Thanks to Efih for the cover concept.

Thanks to all our friends and partners who have prayed and waited for the once "unpublished" book that they knew only by its title.

I remember my late Dad, Deacon Kunle Odulaja who counselled me continually: "Keep on writing." Thanks to my Mum, Pastor Esther Olulaja, for her care, especially during the early years.

I am deeply grateful to the wife of my youth, Linda. Thanks for walking with me on this unusual path, not knowing at times where we were heading but confident in the One we are following. Destiny, Daniel, you are truly the best!

Now unto the King eternal, immortal, invisible, the only wise God, the soon and coming Lord, the giver of grace, the imparter of life, be honour and glory for ever and ever. Amen.

TOKUNBO EMMANUEL
NOVEMBER 2002

*PS: I want to specially acknowledge the timeliness of Dr. Bill Hamon's new book, **The Day of the Saints**. As I read through its pages a few days ago (December 15) I encountered the message of **Run Church Run!** all over again. It was quite encouraging to have a confirmation of some of the things God had revealed in me from an older and more experienced apostle-prophet. God's determination to bring His purpose to a final close in these last moments of destiny is beyond question, for the Spirit of God has birthed these books (and others, I believe) to convey this intent. It was necessary for this matter to be established by the testimony of two or three books." (2 Corinthians 13:1; see also chapter 9 of this book).*

*For a reinforced understanding of the message of **Run Church Run!**, I heartily recommend **The Day of the Saints**.*

FOREWORD

In his latest book, Tokunbo Emmanuel shares insights that have been lodged in his heart since university days. Although these insights have matured and developed over the years, they still retain their initial vigour and freshness and come across with a vibrancy that challenges lethargy in the church and confronts apathy in the lives of individual believers.

Tokunbo is a motivator who writes with a passion, consistently backing up his arguments with exhortations from Scripture. His zeal for restoration in the church and for evangelism in the nations creates a wise balance that makes his call for kingdom advance all the more authentic. He sets his appeal in the context of Christ's second coming, believing that a quickening of spiritual pace on the earth will hasten the Lord's return from heaven. He makes his case for *increasable imminency* by distinguishing between *chronos* and *kairos*, the concepts of time in Scripture.

I commend this book to all who are prepared to think afresh about the church's mission and to back up their thoughts with actions. I can promise you an exciting read, though not always a comfortable one.

I have known Toks for most of the time he has been back in the UK since receiving his university education in Nigeria. I have always appreciated his enthusiasm and sensitivity and now benefit personally from his long-standing desire to develop a Christ-like commitment to servant-hood as we work together in the local church.

HUGH OSGOOD
CORNERSTONE CHRISTIAN CENTRE, UK

AUTHOR'S PREFACE

The mandate to write this book came after organising two mission outreaches for students in Nigeria. *Holiday Outreach '91* and the subsequent year's programme were fruits of a vision to hold a "conference and crusade in the same town, winning the whole town." I am not writing about the outreaches *per se*. Rather, the revelations, convictions and burden that gave birth to them, as well as the prophetic understandings that came during their preparation are relevant for today·

Run Church Run! is a passionate message and not an intellectual thesis. It brings together and summarises the "words" that the Spirit has deposited and developed in me over the years since conversion.

While I have had the opportunity to share many of these messages through preaching, I am aware that the primary outlet God has given me as a "voice" in His kingdom is the *writing ministry*. Hence the persuasion that *Run Church Run!* is a book with a mission. These words are bound to stir up something in you and connect you to God's purpose for your life.

I can appreciate why God has "delayed" the release of *Run Church Run!* until now (I hope you will too when you start reading). Its message has been reserved for a crucial season of God's unprecedented move: the raising up of a refined and resolute people impassioned by the Father's eternal purpose. My earnest prayer is that we all will find our place in His overall agenda.

It is always my desire to communicate revelation in a manner that any believer can comprehend. Hence the many scripture references and occasional repetitions. If you read *Run Church Run!* with an open Bible and open mind, understanding it would not be a problem. The Holy Spirit will stand by you and impress the word upon your heart. I hope the review questions at the end of the book will be helpful as well.

Feel God's heartbeat! Hear His call! My earnest prayer is that we will all buckle our spiritual shoes and *run* to the ends of the earth with the mandate He has placed upon our lives.

"Ready when you are," says the Lord of hosts!

INTRODUCTION

A fresh anointing of the Holy Spirit is coming upon the Church today. The anointing is already here! It is an anointing to *run*. The anointing imparts strength - and strength is needed in our spiritual race. We cannot afford to be spiritually unfit for the race ahead of us.

As we approach the end of the age of grace, a clear observation is that many in the Church have grown weary, cold and somewhat ineffective (see Matthew 24:12; Revelation 3:15,16). Even young people, the workforce of the end-time Church, are wanting for inner strength. A lack of spiritual direction has sapped the strength of many. The glory of young men ought to be divine strength for divine exploits. But what do we see? Insufficient passion. Little aggression. Short-lived drive. Hardly any exploit. "The young men shall utterly fall", the Bible says (Isaiah 40:30 KJV).

In spite of all these, there is still hope.

> "...But they that wait upon the LORD shall renew their strength... they shall *run*, and not be weary" (Isaiah 40:31 KJV *emphasis added*).

Here is the good news: upon every sincerely hungry believer will come a divine infusion of strength in these last days. Strength to run the course of God's commandments! From henceforth and until the coming of Christ, we shall run the race God set for us and not be weary! This is the will and desire of God.

In many individual lives and congregations, this divine strength is already evident. In others, it is still on its way. Whatever your position, this endowment is your portion! God "gives strength to the weary and increases the power of the weak" (Isaiah 40:29).

Time is speeding up to its end. The One who created time has decreed *a time* when time will cease to be.

Now, if God desires to strengthen us, we need to be ready to receive His strength and utilise it appropriately. We must be found running with His agenda and not our own.

In order for us to co-operate with God's plan for these final days, we need to answer some basic questions. *Why* do we need to *run*? To *where* are we running? Why is it important for us to "run in such a way as to get the prize"? Why is the Holy Spirit seeking to increase our momentum on the race-track of life? How shall this increase come and how shall it affect the Church? This book, by the grace of God, will give answers to these and many other questions.

The Lord has a message for the Church and it must be delivered promptly and received reverently. Time is speeding up to its end. The One who created time has decreed *a time* when time will cease to be. We that find ourselves in the realm of time need to be "redeeming the time". *It is time to run!* We must not only run, but must run *speedily* to the end and obtain the prize.

I trust the Holy Spirit to use this book to quicken every reader. His word to the Church at this hour is quite simple: *Run Church Run!*

PART 1

THE IMPORTANCE
OF PURPOSE

1 | REDISCOVERING THE GOD OF PURPOSE

Run for fun!

I once saw this caption in the room of a 10-year old girl. On the poster, an artist had drawn a happy youngster skipping away with a wide smile on her face. For this little girl, life could not be more exciting.

Run for fun! As I fixed my gaze upon this poster and its interesting inscription, the spotlight of my thoughts started to shift. The girl was no more the subject matter. Instead, I began to think about the Church of Jesus Christ.

Run for fun?

Running for nothing?

Active but not productive?

Purpose! Purpose! Purpose!

Just like "Pleasure without measure," *Run for fun!* may have poetical rhythm, but it certainly lacks spiritual meaning. It can produce action, but surely no direction. It may fascinate the carnally-minded, but will nauseate the spiritual. *Run for fun!* is a caption that must only be found in the rooms of 10-year old children!

Only 10-year old children? According to historical documentation, the Church of Jesus Christ, inaugurated on the day of Pentecost, is about 2000 years old. Nonetheless, on the walls of our beautiful cathedrals and conference halls can be found nicely decorated *Run for fun!* plaques, posters and pictures.

Running for nothing? There is an abundance of activity, programmes and services going on in the Church today. As helpful as some of these are, we still need to ask ourselves some pertinent questions:

Are we executing God's purpose for our generation?

*Are we doing His will, all that is in **His** heart and mind?*

Are we fulfilling God's Agenda or ours?

Are we carrying out our divine mandate to mature the Church and reach the world?

Are we living the answer to Christ's plea for unity amongst the believers?

Is God glorified in our worship?

Are we intelligently advancing the Kingdom of God?

Purpose! Purpose! Purpose!

An exertion of energy without any movement towards a specific destination is not considered as work done. Like Israel in the wilderness (see Deuteronomy 2:1-3), it is possible to endlessly go round a particular point of religious stagnation and not make any significant progress towards the land of promise.

God will only reward work that directly advances *His* purposes. We cannot afford to do our own thing and ignore the Spirit's beckoning. There is, therefore, an urgent need to rediscover God's purpose for the Church, what *He* wants us to do and how *He* wants us to do it. We need to understand that our God is a God of purpose and that He has ordained an end-time programme for the world in which we live.

THE GOD OF PURPOSE

God is not a *Run for fun!* God. Everything He does is for a reason and He carries them out in their due season. All His actions have their root in His predetermined counsel.

Whatever God thinks (and concludes upon), He purposes.

Whatever God purposes, He speaks.

Whatever God speaks, He performs.

This is why God's *Word* can never go unfulfilled.

> "So is my word that goes out from my mouth: It will not return to me empty,

> *but will accomplish what I desire and*
> *achieve the purpose for which I sent*
> *it"* (Isaiah 55:11 *emphasis added*).

This is why God's *thoughts* can never be hindered.

> "I know that thou canst do everything,
> and that *no thought can be withholden*
> *from thee"* (Job 42:2 KJV *emphasis added*).

This is also why God's *purposes* can never be thwarted.

> "Surely, *as I have planned, so it will be,*
> and *as I have purposed, so it will stand...*
> For the LORD Almighty has *purposed,*
> and who can thwart him? His hand is
> stretched out, and who can turn it
> back?" (Isaiah 14:24,27 *emphasis added*).

It is possible to endlessly go round a particular point of religious stagnation and not make any significant progress towards the land of promise.

If we, the Church, are going to fully accomplish heaven's divine mandate, we must possess, more than ever, a consciousness of the purpose *for* the mandate. We cannot claim to be involved in God's work if we do not know what the work fully entails. We need a revelation of the *purposes* of God and the *God* of purpose. A revelation of purpose will inevitably motivate effective worship, outreach and ministry.

THE BOUNDARIES OF PURPOSE

Remember this sequence:

God's *thoughts* become God's *purposes*.

God's *purposes* become God's *words*.

God's *words* become God's *work*.

Our God is a God of words and work. He speaks and He acts. Both His word and work have their root in His purposes. You can never find God saying or doing anything aimlessly. Whatever God is currently doing has already been done - in the realm of predestination and proclamation. He "calls things that are not as though they were".

In the beginning, according to His everlasting purpose in creation, God worked for six days, completed His work and thereafter rested. He demonstrated an important principle here; that purpose defines limits and boundaries. Wherever purpose is specific, there will always be a *beginning* and an *ending*. The creation of the heavens and the earth was not an indefinite task that had no visible end. Rather, it was a *specific* project that had *specific* targets. God, therefore, knew when to rest - after all the *specific* objectives for creation were carried out successfully.

Jesus Christ also demonstrated this same principle when He said on the cross, "It is finished". He knew what He came to do in the world and when the assignment was accomplished.

Paul, conscious of God's purpose for his life, said "I consider my life worth nothing to me, if only I may *finish* the race and *complete* the task the Lord Jesus has given me - the task of testifying to the gospel of God's grace" (Acts 20:24 *emphasis added*). Near the end of his life, he wrote to his son in the faith, Timothy, and said, "I have fought the good fight, I have *finished* the race, I have kept the faith" (2 Timothy 4:7).

If we, then, are involved in God's work, we should be able to demonstrate the same principle of purpose. What exactly is the Church ordained to do in the world? How much of the work entrusted into our hands has been done? How much remains undone? With respect to *finishing* what God started, are we progressing, regressing or stagnating? More than ever, we need to evaluate our work in the light of God's word.

ORIGINAL PURPOSE

When God created man and transferred upon him the "authority to rule" all created things, there was an end in view. This end included the emergence of a people united under the Lordship of Jesus Christ, the Son of God. Adam's descendants were going to know and worship God. Man was ordained to live to the praise of God's glory and operate the principles of His Kingdom. To God, through Christ, would belong all supremacy, for "all things were made by Him and for Him" (Colossians 1:16-18). With these in mind, God, during creation, made a statement of purpose and went ahead to carry it out:

> "Then God said, 'Let us make man in our image, in our likeness, and let them rule... So God created man in his own image, male and female He created them... God blessed them and said to them, 'Be fruitful and increase in number; fill the earth and subdue it. Rule over the fish of the sea and the birds of the air and over every living creature that moves on the ground... I give you [everything]...' and it was so" (Genesis 1:26-31).

God purposed.

God pronounced.

God performed.

He was focused, specific and purpose-driven.

> "Thus the heavens and the earth were *completed* in all their vast array. By the seventh day, God had *finished* the work he had been doing; so on the seventh day he rested from all his work" (Genesis 2:1,2 *emphasis added*).

The original purpose was set in motion and man began to walk in the light of it. The life of God

permeated man's existence and there was complete
unity between the Creator and His creation.

**With respect to *finishing*
what God started,
are we progressing,
regressing or stagnating?**

God was resting from *His* work and man was
working *in* God's rest. Caring for the garden
(Genesis 2:15) and naming of the animals (Genesis
2:19,20) were all done in the strength and wisdom
of God. Adam did not need to strive in the flesh.
This was the beginning of purpose. The ending of
it was going to include all of Adam's seed walking
and working in union with God, with the world
completely replenished, developed and subdued.

THE FATHER AT WORK:
PURPOSE, PLAN AND PROPHECY

God worked and rested thereafter. But, we all
know what subsequently happened in the Garden
of Eden.

The serpent deceived the woman and she,
together with her husband, ate the fruit God commanded them not to eat (Genesis 2:17,18; 3:6). The
moment they disobeyed God, they discovered how
naked they were without His covering. They were
thrust into fear and agitation. They forfeited their

right to rule the earth. Needless to say, this act of disobedience momentarily interrupted God's purpose for man to grow into a community of rulers and worshippers. Man's "right to rule" was handed over to God's enemy, the devil. The divine nature he once possessed was traded away for a bite of fruit. God's rest had to be "suspended" because His purpose had been affected. He had to start working again, all in the context of His purpose that cannot but stand forever.

God's original purpose did not change. His intentions for man to rule and dominate were still intact. However, He did not just redo His purpose by speaking it to pass. Instead, He devised a plan and pronounced it in advance.

> "And I will put enmity between thee [the devil] and the woman, and between thy seed and here seed; it shall bruise thy head and thou shalt bruise his heel" (Genesis 3:15 KJV).

Note this important truth: Before the fall of man, God will purpose a thing, pronounce it and perform it, the pronouncement being the performance.

> "And God said, let there be... and there was".

However, since the fall of man, God purposes a thing, devises a plan for its accomplishment, pronounces His plan, and thereafter, performs His *pronounced* plan. The Genesis 3:15 programme that God proclaimed in the Garden of Eden was the birthday of prophecy. It had its root in God's unchangeable purpose.

True prophecies are eternally binding because they originate from God's mind and heart. Whatever God plans and speaks is forever settled in the archives of heaven.

JESUS CHRIST AT WORK: REDEMPTION

The prophecy in Eden pointed to the manifestation of Jesus Christ as the "seed" of the woman that would bruise the head of Satan. The purpose of this manifestation was for the reestablishment of God's purpose - the redemption of man and the restoration of his authority to rule over God's creation.

Many other prophecies went ahead of Christ throughout the Old Testament. None of them were idle words. At the fullness of time, Jesus Christ came to destroy the works of the devil and to fulfil the intentions of God, as it is written:

> "When Christ came into the world, he said: 'Here I am - it is written about me in the scroll - I have come to do your will, O God'" (Hebrews 10:5-7).

The coming of Christ into the world had its root in the divine plan (God's programme):

> "When Christ came into the world."

It had its root in prophecy (God's documented pronouncement):

"it is written about me in the scroll."

And it was rooted in purpose (God's will).

"I have come to do your will, O God."

Christ once said, "My Father is always at his work to this very day, and I, too, am working" (John 5:17). Again He said, "I have come down not to do my will but to do the will of him who sent me" (John 6:38). It was this will of the Father, the original plan and purpose, that necessitated Christ's death upon the cross. He resisted every temptation to evade crucifixion. His prayer of submission in Gethsemane, with blood dripping from His eyebrows, was, "not my will, but yours be done." He laid down His life as an eternal sacrifice for sin, thus accomplishing His part in the divine counsel

Like His Father, Christ did not rest until He finished His part of the work.

He was focused.

He was committed.

He was successful.

THE SPIRIT AT WORK: INNAUGRATION

Now, imagine an eternal relay race; a race of purpose that started from the Garden of Eden. The winning team is the Divine Trinity. The Father started the race and handed over the baton to the Son, and the Son to the Holy Spirit.

Jesus Christ said it would benefit His disciples if He went back to heaven. Since He had finished His work, there was no reason for Him to stay in the world any longer. He said, "Unless I go away, the Counsellor will not come to you; but if I go, I will send him to you" (John 16:7). Purpose demanded that He left and that the Holy Spirit came.

Sure enough, because of purpose, the Holy Spirit came upon the waiting believers on the day of Pentecost.

His coming had its root in *purpose*.

> "When he comes, he will convict the world of guilt in regard to sin and righteousness and judgement... *He will not speak on his own*; he will speak only what he hears..." (John 16:8,13 *emphasis added*).

His coming had its root in *prophecy*.

> "*This is what was spoken by the prophet Joel*: 'In the last days, God says, I will pour out my Spirit on all people...'" (Acts 2:16,17 *emphasis added*; compare with Joel 2:28-ff)

The Holy Spirit came to work and not to play. He came to give birth to the Church and thereafter, through the Church, bring an end to the dispensation of grace.

THE CHURCH AT WORK: CONSUMMATION

The spiritual birth of the Church was the commencement of the Spirit's part of God's work on earth (His time to be in the forefront of heaven's earthly activity). The role of the Church since then has been the continuation of this work in partnership with the Holy Spirit. The ultimate aim is the rounding up of all things and the fulfilment of all prophecies.

The birth and existence of the Church has its root in God's purpose, programme, plan and prophecies.

The Church's purpose today is no different from the Father's.

The Church's purpose today is no different from the Son's.

The Church's purpose today is no different from the Holy Spirit's.

The Church of Jesus Christ, of which you and I are a part, has a reason for being here. We have a message to preach and a generation to reach. We have a Kingdom life to live and a Kingdom love to exhibit. We have a world to deliver unto our Lord and King.

Our Saviour made an important statement before He left the earth. He said, "Just as the Father sent me, so send I you" (John 20:21).

"Just as the Father sent me" means for the same reason; for the same purpose; in the same way; in the same manner.

"So send I you" means for this same reason; for this same purpose; in this same way; in this same manner.

We ought to do the works that Christ did.

We ought to live the life that Christ lived.

We ought to have the zeal that Christ had.

We ought to pray the prayers that Christ prayed.

We ought to see the results that Christ saw.

We have been sent into the world *just as* Christ was sent into the world, to do the works that He did and live for the purpose for which he lived.

We have a message to preach and a generation to reach. We have a Kingdom life to live and a Kingdom love to exhibit.

As the Father did not rest until He finished *His* work, and the Son did not rest until He finished *His* work, we cannot afford to sleep in God's vineyard until *our* mandate is fulfilled. The Holy Spirit, you can be sure, will not allow us the luxury.

We cannot afford to *Run for fun!*

We must not rest until we do our best.

We need to focus on the reason for our being and pursue it with every ounce of strength that we have.

2 | ADVANCING PURPOSE BY FORCE (I)

The essence of *purpose* is its accomplishment.

The essence of a *plan* is its execution.

The essence of *prophecy* is its fulfilment.

Purpose, plans and prophecy are all pointless if they have nothing specific to achieve. In the same vein, any spiritual activity outside the sphere of purpose can be considered an eternal waste. God does not satisfy Himself with mere *pronouncements* of His will. There has to "be a *performance* of those things which were [spoken by] the Lord" (Luke 1:45 KJV *emphasis added*).

It is possible to receive a prophecy from God and, perhaps because of a shallow understanding of its root in purpose, do nothing with it. Although we cannot bring God's Word to pass in our own strength, we are, however, expected to co-operate with Him for its fulfilment. We must "fight the good fight" with every prophecy that we receive from God (2 Timothy 1:18). Identifying with the purpose of God's pronouncements will motivate the fight and ensure the victory.

"THE KINGDOM OF GOD SUFFERETH VIOLENCE"

We are part of God's army, fighting for the advancement of His kingdom. There is, at the same time, a master schemer in the world that is diligently seeking for ways to weaken and side-track those who fight for the Lord. The physical fulfilment of God's will, therefore, does not come that easily at times, even though they are already done when He pronounces them. (This is so, at least, from our point of view). An understanding of this truth is imperative if we are going to advance God's purpose in our generation.

If there is nobody willing to sacrifice personal desires and agendas for the sake of accomplishing God's will (someone through whom God can execute His counsel), the fulfilment will either be delayed or hindered entirely. Prophecies, plans and strategies are impotent without strong people who will work them out. That is why God will always raise up a man to fulfil His intentions. God

Himself said, "From the east I summon a bird of prey; from a far-off land, *a man to fulfil my purpose*" (Isaiah 46:11 *emphasis added*).

When God was ready to displace Eli as high priest in Israel, He hinted on the reason why Samuel was His preferred choice. God said, "I will raise up for myself a faithful priest, *who will do according to what is in my heart and mind*" (1 Samuel 2:35 *emphasis added*). He testified about David as well, saying, "I have found David the son of Jesse, a man after mine own heart, *which shall fulfil all my will*" (Acts 13:22 *emphasis added*; see also 1 Samuel 13:14 KJV).

This truth is further portrayed in the following words of Christ:

> "From the days of John the Baptist until now the kingdom of heaven has been forcefully advancing, and forceful men lay hold of it. For all the Prophets and the Law prophesied until John". (Matthew 11:12,13).

Notice the two time-spans in this text - *before* the days of John the Baptist and *after* the days of John the Baptist.

What happened *before* the days of John the Baptist? *All the Prophets and the Law prophesied **until** John.*

Before John the Baptist appeared on the shores of Galilee with a message of repentance, there was an abundance of prophecies about the Christ who was to come. Virtually all the prophets, in one form or the other, spoke about God's plan to send Israel a deliverer. They prophesied about the One who was coming to redeem man from sin and death. Burdened with a desire for the purposes of God's heart, "holy men of God spake as they were moved by the Holy Ghost" (2 Peter 1:21 KJV). They even "searched intently and with the greatest care, trying to find out the time and circumstances to which the Spirit of Christ in them was pointing when he predicted the sufferings of Christ and the glories that would follow" (1 Peter 1:10,11).

Thank God for prophecies! They foretell what God has in mind to do. They inspire hope and expectation. However, if John did not come to prepare the way of the Lord, the prophecies would have remained as prophecies and not become realities.

Prophecies, plans and strategies are impotent without strong people who will work them out.

After many centuries of prediction by "all the Prophets and the Law", there followed a period of 400 years of silence and stagnation. Nobody heard from heaven and nothing happened on earth. Prophecies ceased and their fulfilment lingered.

When the time was right, God had to send John, a "forceful man", to advance His word. This unusual man who dwelt in uncommon places and ate strange food, broke all the traditions of his time and advanced the purpose of God. It takes an unusual man to stand against the usual order of things.

God used John as a voice in the wilderness to prepare the way for the coming of Christ, so that all that was in His heart, the countless prophecies about the Messiah, may come to fruition.

Notice further from the text that John is not supposed to be the only forceful man advancing God's purpose. Christ spoke of "forceful men" laying hold of the kingdom *from the days of John the Baptist until now*. The implication of this is that the purpose of God for our time and day has to be advanced by forceful people with aggressive spirits. Because you and I are living in the second time span - *after* the day of John the Baptist - heaven is counting on us to forcefully advance the kingdom of God and the counsels in God's heart.

> **It takes an unusual man to stand against the usual order of things.**

GOD IS A FORCEFUL GOD

If there is anyone consumed with a passion for purpose, it is God Himself. He cannot allow His word to remain passive for too long. Sooner or later, He will take action - violent action at times - to advance His purpose. Our God is a forceful God. He is called "a man of war" (see Exodus 15:3 KJV).

When the execution of prophecy is delayed for one reason or another, God will step in to bring them to pass by Himself. And when God intervenes, who can hinder him? When He stretches forth His hand, who can turn it back? Isaiah's vision of God's passion for and commitment to purpose is striking:

> "Who is this coming from Edom, from Bozrah, with his garments stained crimson? Who is this, robed in splendor, striding forward in the greatness of his strength? 'It is I, speaking in righteousness, mighty to save.' Why are your garments red, like those of one treading the winepress? 'I have trodden the winepress *alone*; from the nations *no one was with me*... I looked, but *there was no one to help*, I was appalled that *no one gave support*; so *my own arm worked* salvation for me, and *my own wrath sustained* me. I trampled the nations in my anger; in my wrath I made them drunk and poured their blood on the ground.'" (Isaiah 63:1-3,5,6 *emphasis added*).

God can do almost anything, in line with His character and principles, to perform His word. His preferred action, though, has always been to painstakingly look for a man or woman, and send such to carry out His plan. The call of Moses further illustrates this concept.

"The LORD said [to Moses], '*I have seen* the misery of my people in Egypt. *I have heard* them crying out because of their slave drivers, and *I am concerned* about their suffering. So *I have come down* to rescue them from the hand of the Egyptians and to bring them up out of that land into a good and spacious land, a land flowing with milk and honey... So now, go. *I am sending you* to Pharaoh to bring my people the Israelites out of Egypt'" (Exodus 3:7-10).

God's people were suffering under Egyptian bondage and deliverance was not forthcoming. Long before this time, a prediction was made about their exodus from Egypt (see Genesis 15:12-14). Even though the time for the fulfilment of this prophecy was due, the authenticity of the prediction alone did not activate their deliverance. Why did Israel spend an extra thirty years in Egypt, four hundred and thirty years instead of four hundred (compare Genesis 15:12-14 with Exodus 12:40,41)? Perhaps they were contented with the garlic of Egypt and did not see the need to cry out to God; perhaps there was no-one God could use to fulfil prophecy. Whatever the reason, God was deeply concerned.

When Israel eventually cried out for deliverance, the Lord made a move to execute His word.

God said, "*I* have *seen* my people."

God said, "*I* have *heard* my people."

God said, "*I* am *concerned* about my people."

God said, "*I* have *come down* to save my people."

God "came down" to advance His purpose. And what was the result? The commissioning of Moses, the man through whom God would bring both prophecy and purpose to pass. He laid His hands forcefully on Moses, put a divine burden upon his, and used Him to deliver Israel from bondage.

FEELING GOD'S HEARTBEAT

Since the time of John the Baptist until now, the kingdom of heaven has been forcefully advancing. God has never settled for anything less than the total fulfilment of His purposes. He is the number one Forceful Man advancing the original divine mandate.

Different people throughout the ages have felt God's heartbeat and identified with His desire for the reign of righteousness in the earth. Paul felt the pulse of God and was driven to the ends of the earth as a light to the Gentiles. Martin Luther was feeling the heart of God when, against the religious practices of his day, he maintained his stand on the revelation of God's word - that the just shall live by faith and not by lifeless rituals. All the revivalists that God had ever used were forceful men and women acquainted with the heart of God. They identified with His purposes and developed His passion. If the Lord will do anything significant through us today, we need to know His heart and embrace His passion.

God has graciously brought me close to the place where I could feel the beat of purpose in His heart. It is not a passive what-will-be-will-be pulsation, but a violent emission of holy zeal for the fulfilment of His prophecies and purposes. It is "the zeal of the Lord", the Bible says, that accomplishes things in the Kingdom.

> **All the revivalists that God had ever used were forceful men and women acquainted with the heart of God.**

You cannot get close to the heart of God and remain the same. You cannot catch the fire of God's holy love and live a mediocre life that neither affects heaven or hell. Your whole life and desires will turn around completely. Could it be possible that a lot of believers are lukewarm today because they have not had a direct encounter with the heart of God?

There is a tone of seriousness in the voice of the angel who *"swore* by him who lives forever and ever... and said, 'There will be no more delay! But in the days when the seventh angel is about to sound his trumpet, *the mystery of God will be accomplished, just as he announced to his servants the prophets'"* (Revelation 10:6,7 *emphasis added*). More than ever, God is watching over *all* His word and He is ready to bring it to pass no matter the cost.

THREE FORCEFUL RESOLUTIONS

During the first eight months of 1991, while preparing to hold a mission-oriented programme for students during the long holiday, God opened up His heart and shared some things with me that radically changed my life. He poured insight and revelation into my spirit about His agenda for this generation and the need to speed up His purpose. I was made to observe and understand how, in many respects, the Church's interest was on things other than the accomplishment of purpose. I was also showed some of the things God was determined to do in order to forcefully advance His will.

It was my final year as a computer science student at the *Obafemi Awolowo University*, Nigeria West Africa, and in the previous year (1990) I had received an instruction to gather students together for a "conference and crusade at the same place." Together with some friends, we went all out to pursue the vision of *Holiday Outreach 1991 (HO '91, as we called it)*. Even though the concept of convening students for a three-week long outreach was unpopular at the time, *HO '91* was borne out of prophetic understanding. God's intention was that a lot of missionaries, students and young people in particular, would go forth from Nigeria to reach the nations of the earth. God was going to accomplish this in spite of the obvious lack of awareness about missions amongst the young at that time and a completely different emphasis by the Church in general.

It was in this context that God shared with me what I have called *three forceful resolutions* - some things He was ready to do in order to advance His purpose among the Nigerian youth and a passive Church. Since they were all based on Scripture, their application goes beyond the situation prevailing in the Church in Nigeria at that time (1991).

These resolutions came to me with such force and authority and their effect has stayed with me since then. I pray that your life will be affected in a positive way as you read.

RESOLUTION #1

This was the first word the Lord spoke in my heart:

> "If it has to take the blood of a man to advance my purpose on the earth, I will gladly take it"

What is the meaning of this hard saying?

First note the phrase *my purpose*. In the previous chapter, we established that God has a purpose and plan for man that started in the Garden of Eden. After man's fall, this purpose remained the same but a plan was drawn up for its accomplishment. The nucleus of this plan was the death and resurrection of Jesus Christ. The continuation and eventual fulfilment of this plan was entrusted to the Church of God in the earth.

A vital part of this eternal purpose, as it pertains to the Church today, is to reach the ends of the earth with the gospel and prepare for the second coming of Christ.

The Father started this work.

Jesus Christ continued the work.

The Holy Spirit is now at work *through* the Church.

The Church of Jesus Christ at this present time is in partnership with the Holy Spirit for the completion of this work.

Now, Jesus Christ *specifically* instructed His Church on where to *start* the preaching of the good news ("Jerusalem") and where to *end* ("ends of the earth"). They were told to do this with the help of the Holy Spirit.

> "But you will receive power when the Holy Spirit comes on you; and you will be my witnesses *in Jerusalem,* and *in all Judea* and *Samaria,* and to *the ends of the earth*" (Acts 1:8 *emphasis added*).

This statement of *purpose* from Christ to the Church defined the *scope* of the mandate (Jerusalem, Judea, Samaria and the ends of the earth) and the *strategy* for its accomplishment (power to be witnesses).

The early Church obeyed the Lord's command. They waited for the Holy Spirit and received the promise of power. They started to proclaim, with astounding results, the good news of the Kingdom. They shared with unshakeable conviction the testimony of Christ's resurrection - as far as *Jerusalem* was concerned. The downside of their success in Jerusalem was that they lost sight of the *scope* of their mandate; *Judea, Samaria* and *the ends of the earth* was no more in view. With a misplaced focus, they ceased to advance the purpose of God for the Church.

There was revival in the Church at Jerusalem.

There were miracles in the Church at Jerusalem.

There was healing in the Church at Jerusalem.

There was fellowship in the Church at Jerusalem.

There was growth in the Church at Jerusalem.

Every good thing that any congregation of our time would desire was present in the Church at Jerusalem, except for one thing... the advancement of purpose.

From chapter 1-6 of the Book of Acts, we will read of the Jerusalem revival but not the advancement of the original purpose of God in its fullness - Jerusalem, Judea, Samaria and the uttermost parts of the earth.

The Blood of a Man

God is more interested in the advance of His purpose than in religious parties. The time for partying is after all work has been done.

The early Church could not discern that in spite of their growth, only a "quarter" of Christ's specified will for them was being done. God wanted the church to move beyond their "mountain of success", but they were feasting, and sometimes fighting, on food. Problems will always thrive when purpose is neglected (Proverbs 29:18).

God wanted them to send out missionaries to other cities outside Jerusalem (as the Church in Antioch did years later - Acts 13) but they either could not see the need for this or could not hear the Spirit urging them to do so.

God is more interested in the advance of His purpose than in religious parties. The time for partying is after all work has been done.

God had to act.

God did act.

His action was drastic.

It was the move of a forceful Man of war.

The move was unconventional and painful.

But it was also effective.

God's move was *the blood of a man* - Stephen, the first Christian martyr.

God performed miraculous signs among the people through Stephen, but He also allowed the faithful deacon to be stoned to death by the unbelieving Jews. His death, spearheaded by a young Pharisee, Saul of Tarsus (who later became the Apostle Paul), brought tears to the eyes of the believers but joy to the angels of heaven. Stephen's death advanced the purpose of God beyond Jerusalem and won a standing ovation from the resurrected Christ.

> "'Look', [Stephen] said, 'I see heaven open and the Son of man *standing at the right hand of God'*. At this they covered their ears and, yelling at the top of their voices, they all rushed at him, dragged him out of the city and began to stone him... And Saul was there, giving approval to his death." (Acts 7:56-58; 8:1a *emphasis added*).

Now notice the result of Stephen's death on the Church.

> "*On that day* a great persecution broke out against the Church *at Jerusalem*, and all except the apostles were scattered throughout *Judea and Samaria*" (Acts 8:1 *emphasis added*).

The Bible is very specific in its records. It was the Church *at Jerusalem* that was scattered throughout *Judea and Samaria*, the regions Christ had particularly mentioned in Acts 1:8.

God literally forced the Church into His preordained counsel - Jerusalem, Judea, Samaria and the ends of the earth. The Bible went on to reveal that "those who had been scattered preached the word wherever they went" (Acts 8:4).

Philip, also a deacon like Stephen, went "to a city in *Samaria* and proclaimed the Christ there". The result was that "there was a great joy in that city" (Acts 8:5-8). Afterwards, "when the apostles in Jerusalem heard that Samaria had accepted the word of God, they sent Peter and John to them... Then Peter and John placed their hands on them, and they received the Holy Spirit" (Acts 8:14-17).

In a single, forceful move of God, through the death of a righteous man, the purpose of God advanced from Jerusalem to the surrounding regions of Judea and Samaria. God considered the forceful advance of purpose more important than the temporal mourning of His people. Would the story have been different if before the persecution, the Apostles had organised some missionary out-reaches and sent workers into the cities outside Jerusalem? They had the resources (men and money - Acts 4:32-37; 6:3) but had lost the revela-tion and the motivation.

Application

God may use, and so often does use seemingly bad situations to get us in line with His will for our lives. He has His eyes on the goal and not just the means. He is focused on the future and not just the present. Throughout history, the hand of the Lord has effected progress in ways similar to the above narrative. The blood of the martyr is indeed the seed of harvest in the Church. Would God have to repeat this feat in our day?

Many believers from the so-called "Third-World" nations (myself included) have had to relocate to the West, not just because of economic hardships, but because God had in mind the spread of the gospel in a section of the world that had become a vast mission field. While a few might have caught the vision of why God brought us into "lands of opportunity", there are still many who are missing the purpose of their present location. Even many who presently lead congregations are not properly aligned with the programme of God. What would He have to do again to get us in line?

I am no advocate of death. I am just sharing the word of the Lord. The year that the Lord communicated these things to me, quite a number of precious souls in Nigeria, ministers in particular, crossed over to glory. These were faithful people with fruitful ministries.

The revival and Church unity reported in the *Transformation I* video broke after a minister died. Even in our individual lives, we seem to get serious with God after disaster strikes. Certainly, this is not God's way, but what should He do when we leave Him with no other alternative?

Let us ask ourselves sincere questions. Are our churches and ministries like the Church at Jerusalem? Does our programmes and meetings originate from purpose - God's purpose? Are we merely inward-looking where ministry and money is concerned, unaware of the work of God in other nations?

It is the will of God, I believe, for every congregation to be committed to missions and world evangelism in one way or the other. "The ends of the earth" is the defining scope of our mandate.

It is also God's will for the Church to walk in complete unity. How are we faring with respect to this? Are we living in the entirety of God's revealed truths? Must God, as a matter of necessity, shake us into conformity with His purpose once again? We all need to answer these questions in our hearts before the Lord. Even though our God is gracious and patient, He will not wait indefinitely for the execution of His counsel. After a while, a very long while in many cases, we will have to do His will, or else...

Must God, as a matter of necessity, shake us into conformity with His purpose once again?

3 | ADVANCING PURPOSE BY FORCE (II)

RESOLUTION #2

The second resolution God shared with me, regarding the advancement of His will in the Church can be summarised in the following words:

> "If it has to take you doing something that you have never done before in order to advance my purpose, then do it!"

What does this word imply?

After persecution broke out in the Church at Jerusalem, the believers were scattered abroad and the work of God progressed. The commission of the Church, as stated in Acts 1:8, advanced from a ¼ fulfilment-level to a ¾ fulfilment-level. This was a mark of progress at that point in time, but it was not fulfilment. I shall explain what this means.

The gospel was ordained to reach *the ends of the earth*. The fulfilment of this was the determining factor for the return of Christ (Matthew 24:14). God relied upon the disciples to *run* with the full mandate and complete the task.

For seven years, God waited for the apostles in Jerusalem to move the Church on to the ends of the earth, but, again, nothing was forthcoming from them. The believers were doing a good work in Jerusalem, Judea, Samaria and the surrounding regions, but they did not go any further. They only spoke to people they were familiar with - people from similar backgrounds.

> "Now *those who had been scattered by the persecution in connection with Stephen* travelled a far as Phoenicia, Cyprus and Antioch, *telling the message only to Jews*" (Acts 11:19 *emphasis added*).

Tradition, fear and cultural discrimination hindered the advance of God's Kingdom beyond Jewish boarders. The believers could not see that the ends of the earth included the gentile nations. Ministry within Israelite borders constituted a comfort zone for the early church.

God had to intervene again.

He did so, violently.

God launched Peter into a trance and repeatedly shared the ends-of-the-earth mandate with him in parables (Acts 10:23). He also sent an angel to prepare the heart of Cornelius, a gentile, for the reception of the gospel through Peter (Acts 10:1-8).

In his vision, Peter struggled with the idea of doing something he had never done before - the eating of unclean animals. He labelled reaching out to un-reached areas an unclean task. The response of God was, "Do not call anything impure that God has made clean". Peter tried to choose tradition instead of obedience to God. He tried to justify his stand but his point was overruled. To God, purpose was more important than tradition; obedience was better than sacrifice.

When Peter eventually obeyed the Lord and went to the house of Cornelius, he tried so hard to stick to his known ministry protocol. Obviously, the Holy Spirit was not going to wait. While Peter was still talking, this Gentile household received the gift of salvation and the infilling of the Spirit simultaneously.

Application

Tradition says, "as it was in the beginning, so it is now, and shall forever be. Amen". God does not "Amen" statements like this. Sticking to the old, tried and tested way of doing things may sound safe, predictable and controllable, but it is not always the realm in which God operates. Tradition cannot advance the purposes of God.

The Pharisees in Jesus' day exalted tradition above God's word. The question Jesus asked them was, "Why do you break the command of God for the sake of your tradition?" (Matthew 15:3). In stronger terms, He said, "You have let go of the commands of God and are holding on to the traditions of men... *Thus you nullify the word of God by your tradition* that you have handed down. And you do many things like that." (Mark 7:8,13 *emphasis added*).

Virtually every move of God has been institutionalised by man. They usually start as a movement but end up as monuments. Even now, Pentecostal and Charismatic tradition is threatening the next move of God. Man cannot control revival in much the same way that he cannot control God. True revival is the handiwork of the Almighty.

Whenever an instruction from God demands activity beyond our comfort zone, even though tradition protests, we need to obey. Racial preferences may say "no", but we must say "yes" to God. Tradition will want to discuss with the committee, but like Peter, we need to obey first and discuss later.

As I shared earlier, *Holiday Outreach 1991* was against the norm of the time. Students took up holiday jobs during school breaks and there was nothing like holiday missions. Even though we had not done anything like it before, God gave us grace to see the programme through without yielding to fear, pressure and tradition.

The will of God goes beyond our physical comfort and security. The life of faith that advances God's purpose is not operational in the realms of calculation. God will move forcefully against our "safety measures" if they stand against His will in our lives.

Whenever an instruction from God demands activity beyond our comfort zone, even though tradition protests, we need to obey.

God is calling for much change in the Church today. A reformation of the ecclesiastical order is paramount. Many apostles and prophets, through messages and books, have attempted to expound on the corporate and individual changes necessary for progress in the Kingdom. The underlying truth is that to obey God adequately, change is inevitable. Any resistance to change can delay the purposes of God. It will certainly hinder our effectiveness in executing the kingdom mandate.

The primary place where change and reformation should occur is in our hearts and minds. The primary agents for implementing these are the Spirit and word of God.

Those who have their inner ears tuned to hear the Lord would quickly recognise the need for paradigm shifts in our mindset and ministry practices. If we continue to do the things we have always been doing, we would continue to have the results we have always been having. What God wants is more important than what we *think* He wants.

In the Church today, our comfort zones need to be discomforted.

Our walls of safety that exclude God need to be broken down.

All ease in Zion needs to be disturbed.

The purposes of God *must* be fulfilled.

The people that God will use in our day will of a necessity be tradition-breakers (not troublemakers but tradition-breakers!). They will be determined to live *all* the truths of God. They will have hearts that can receive new, creative, adventurous ideas for the spreading of the gospel to the ends of the earth; and wills to obey at all cost.

RESOLUTION #3

The third resolution God shared with me regarding the advancement of His purpose is contained in the following statement:

> "If it has to take "the sun and the moon" to stand still for total victory, then they will have to stand still".

The background story is the battle between Israel and the unholy alliance formed by five heathen kings (Joshua 10:1-28). Joshua was leading Israel to battle against these allied forces; just as the army of God on earth today, the Church, is in battle against the combined forces of hell.

What God wants is more important than what we *think* He wants.

The purpose of God for Joshua was clearly defined from the onset: the total obliteration of the inhabitants of Canaan, their idols and their customs. The Church also has a clear purpose: to reach every tongue, tribe and nation with the gospel, displacing Satan's rule and establishing the Kingdom of God in the earth.

Joshua and the Israelite army confronted their enemies and in every way, they were winning the battle. The opposition was thrown into panic and confusion. The Israelites were killing them by the sword and God was killing them with hailstones from heaven (verses 9-11).

However, as the battle continued well past afternoon time, the sun was setting on the west side of the battleground. This natural sunset was threatening to halt the massacre of God's enemies. The night was fast approaching which made sustaining the onslaught impracticable.

Joshua could have settled for half victory. After all, a great number of the enemy's soldiers had already been slain. Half victory, however, did not satisfy Joshua. Something stirred up within this violent man. He did not want to postpone the battle for another day. With all the faith he could muster, Joshua commanded the sun and the moon to stand still... and they did.

> "The sun stopped in the middle of the sky and delayed going down about a full day. There has never been a day like it before or since, a day when the LORD listened to a man. Surely the LORD was fighting for Israel!" (Joshua 10:12-14).

As far as purpose and total victory was concerned, the natural order of things constituted a hindrance before Joshua, and God was ready to answer his bold request for them to be put on hold. Again, purpose was of a higher priority than nature. Israel was able to gain total victory over the opposition after this miracle was performed.

Application

From the insight in this story, God pointed out to me that He could put anything on hold if it stands in the way of purpose. He can suspend any law from working for a season if it becomes necessary. Even some ministers and their ministries, the Lord shared, can be put on "hold" for a season if they constitute a roadblock in the way of full maturity in the Body of Christ.

The holiday programme for students that I have been sharing about was held whilst our university was closed down by the ruling government at that time. The closure lasted about eight weeks. God literally put the educational system "on hold" so that His purpose for the programme might be carried out.

I learnt something else during this period. I had just received the above revelations and therefore, had an idea of what was happening. Some believers, however, claimed that God had told them we should pray and choose a date for the re-opening of the university; and that it will re-open without fail. Apparently, the people who "received" this word from God were final year students. They desperately wanted to finish their studies that year and not spend extra months in school. I was not convinced the Lord had spoken because the date they chose preceded the time our programme was due to start. Of course, they prayed but the school was still closed after their chosen date.

The most interesting thing that happened was that the announcement for the reopening of the university was made the day after *Holiday Outreach 1991* ended! I learnt a treasured truth that day: God will rather answer prayers that are in line with *His* purpose than the ones that are only for the pleasing of self. He will rather honour faith that advances *His* Kingdom than mere optimism that advances our earthly empires and desires (see James 4:1-3).

God, in these last days, is looking for bold prayers that He can give answers to. There are so many people praying today but only a few are offering the dangerous, bold and violent prayers that advance the Kingdom of God. Praying in this manner guarantees results. There is nothing like unanswered prayers in the realm of purpose.

> "If you remain in me and my words remain in you (that is, if my purpose and counsel is established in you), *ask whatever you wish, and it will be given you*" (John 15:7 *emphasis added*).

> "Ask of me, and I will make the nations your inheritance, the ends of the earth your possession" (Psalms 2:8).

God will rather answer prayers that are in line with *His* purpose than the ones that are only for the pleasing of self.

God is interested in the total accomplishment of His purpose in our time. He is not satisfied with a job half-done. A ¼ or even ¾ level of accomplishment is not enough. In our generation, the purpose of God must be totally fulfilled. Remember this always:

> *Progress* is not good enough if it becomes a hindrance to total *accomplishment*.

God is going to raise for Himself forceful men and women who will run to the ends of the earth, *fulfilling* and *finishing* the God-given mandate of the Church. Indeed, the entire Church is destined to be on the move at this time. If Jesus Christ will come as He promised, the Church needs to run with holy zeal, advancing the kingdom of God by force. In these last days, all prophecies must come to pass and every mandate fulfilled.

THEN WORD, NOW WORD

Every word of the Lord is alive and powerful. When He speaks, "who can but prophesy?" (Amos 3:8). Even though the resolutions expounded in the last two chapters were received more than ten years ago, they are yet fresh for today. God is *still* interested in advancing His purposes - perhaps now more than ever before.

In the light of the above, I will share one more word the Lord spoke to me on February 2, 1992. As I prepared for Church on this Sunday morning, the Lord visited me in the shower. These were the words He spoke into my spirit:

> You would go to the UK to declare my word, for I am going to walk through my Church to turn the hearts of my people from what they are desiring to what I want them to desire...

I was gripped by this word, to say the least, because the first thing that came to mind upon hearing it was the resolutions discussed above - "the blood of a man", to be precise! Living in Nigeria at the time, I did not know the "condition" of the Church in the UK or the fullness of what God was saying. I could only sense the seriousness in His voice.

Having now lived in the UK for the past ten years, it is my opinion (and that of many ministers I have and have not met) that the Lord is calling for radical change. The word of the Lord is relevant *now*. God is doing a quick and deep work. He wants us to desire *His* desires and pursue *His* pursuits. He is determined to bring us into conformity with His will, even if it means shaking both the heavens and the earth.

A generation of people must urgently arise in the Church today. A people ready to *enforce* the full manifestation of God's kingdom in the earth. A people soaked in the prayers of Christ: "Kingdom of God, come! Will of God, be done!" (Matthew 6:10 *literal paraphrase*). A people flowing in decisive apostolic authority and pointed prophetic revelation. A united people with a united purpose - the consummation of the will of God.

They must arise and they *are* arising. They seek no fame but desire only to glorify His name. They seek no man-given position for God has already positioned them in Christ. They seek no earthly kingdom for their God has prepared a heavenly city for them (Hebrews 11:15,16). They are young, they are old; they are black, they are white; they are male, they are female; they are many and they are one - *in* Christ and *for* Christ.

Are you a part?

Will you run?

PART 2

THE PATH
OF TRANSFORMATION

4 | WHY IS CHRIST STILL SITTING IN HEAVEN?

From the lips of the most purposeful man who ever lived came these words:

> "I am the Alpha and the Omega... who is, and who was and who is to come, the Almighty... I am the Living One; I was dead and behold I am alive for ever and ever!" (Revelation 1:8,18).

Jesus Christ *was*, He *is* and He *is to come*. He lives in all three dimensions of eternity. Jesus lived, died and lives for a purpose.

He came to save the world from sin. He is presently "saving" in heaven because "He always lives to intercede for" us (Hebrews 7:25). He will

come again to save the Church from the wrath
to come.

Throughout His earthly existence, Jesus was
consumed with only one passion: to *do* the will of
the Father and to *finish* His work. This was his
food, His motivation and His reason for living
(John 4:34). He had no time to play around. He
made sure that He worked while He could, aware
that "night-time" was coming when He would not
be able to work.

When Christ comes the second time, it shall also
be with a passion to *finish* the counsels of God. He
shall come for the Church that He lived, died and is
alive for. In the meantime, our Saviour is in
heaven, still concerned about the purposes of God
here on earth. This is the very reason why He is
interceding for us everyday.

ENTHRONED WITH PASSION

After Christ gave His final instructions to the
disciples, "He was taken up into heaven and he sat
at the right hand of God" (Mark 16:19). He sat
down enthroned in majesty. He resumed His position of glory in heaven having completed His task
on earth.

When you finish a hard job, you long for somewhere to rest, a place of refreshment. Christ dis-
charged the toughest work any man can ever
embark upon, went into heaven, and sat down on
His throne beside the Father. However, our Lord

did not start an eternal holiday in heaven. He did not switch into inactivity. He did not have spiritual retirement in mind when He ascended on high. Jesus is not on vacation in the heavens.

As we have read, Christ still lives to make intercession on our behalf (Hebrews 7:25). He "is at the right hand of God and is also interceding for us" (Romans 8:34). Intercession is work - hard work. Although Christ finished *His work* on earth, He is still involved in *The Work* in heaven.

When Christ comes the second time, it shall also be with a passion to *finish* the counsels of God.

Christ is still consumed with passion - a passion to see the completion of God's eternal purpose. He is earnestly looking forward to that time when He will hand over the Kingdoms of this world to God the Father, having "destroyed all dominion, authority and power" (see 1 Corinthians 15:20-28). This passion does not allow for an indifferent attitude to God's purpose. It prevails over an "after-all-I-have-finished-my-part" mindset. So far there is work to be done, Christ cannot sit on His throne unconcerned.

Intercession accomplishes the will of God. It is one of the primary instruments given to believers to advance God's purposes and enforce His prophecies. Christ prayed throughout His earthly ministry. He prayed for Peter in the time of temptation. He prayed for the Church that would be left in the world (John 17). He is still praying for us today. He is still working. Intercession motivated by passion and rooted in purpose guarantees powerful results.

SITTING AND STANDING

The very moment Christ got to heaven, He started to pray for His Body on earth. He knew that He had sent innocent sheep into the midst of deadly wolves. He had a first-hand experience of the opposition they would confront and He tried to prepare them for the inevitable (John 15:20,21; 16:2-4). If the infant Church was going to accomplish the ancient mission, He needed to be involved with them through intercession.

Pentecost was no doubt a day of excitement for Christ in heaven! The Holy Spirit, like a mighty rushing wind, came upon the waiting believers in answer to the Lord's request from the Father (John 14:16). Jesus had told his disciples not to start the task of preaching the word until the Holy Spirit came upon them. Only after the Spirit descends would there be a smooth transition into the Church age. No doubt, work accelerated on this memorable day as 3,000 people were added to the church after Peter's Spirit-energised message.

The expectation of Christ was that the Church would take the message of salvation to the nations of the earth just as He had commanded them in His parting words. He waited for the Church to move out of Jerusalem and fulfil their mandate. However, as we have discussed in previous chapters, the Church refused to advance beyond Jerusalem.

Jesus Christ was sitting in heaven quite all right, but He was a bit "uncomfortable". He noticed how quickly His disciples forgot a vital lesson he had taught them: that they were called to be *pioneers* and not *settlers*. He had also taught them to be focused on purpose; to desire not just progress in ministry, but more importantly, the accomplishment of purpose.

Many times Christ had to leave a booming revival scene to take the message of the Kingdom to other needy regions (see Luke 4:42-44). He expected the Apostles to recall those instances because the Holy Spirit was with them to remind them. They were expected to resist the temptation of concentrating only on Jerusalem and spread the word in other communities. Sadly, the growing Church forgot these vital lessons. Fear and tradition kept them out of tune with the Holy Spirit. In the parameters of purpose, they settled on a spiritual plateau.

Jesus Christ, out of passion (not agitation), could hardly sit still on His throne. In the same way that He once told the disciples, "Have I been so long with you, and yet hast thou not known me?" (John 14:9 KJV), the voice of the Lord could nearly be heard from heaven, "Must I come down again to teach you that you are in the world for a purpose and not a party!"

He did "come down" *in the spirit* a couple of times and still does so today. He "came", for instance, to arrest and commission Saul of Tarsus on the road to Damascus. At another instance, He "came" to give John, the beloved, visions of the future. Many people in around the world, especially in Arab countries and other "closed" nations, have testified to seeing the Lord call them into the faith. Yes, Christ, because of His passion for God's purpose, has had to "stand up" from His heavenly seat a number of times. Stephen, the martyr, saw Him "standing" in heaven and many are still seeing Him today in the spirit.

"THE LORD SAID UNTO MY LORD"

The zeal of God is evident in the life of Christ (see John 2:12-17). Even as a little boy, He was bent on doing His heavenly Father's will (see Luke 2:41-51). He has shown us how to love and live for the Father and expects us to follow His footsteps.

Many times Christ had to leave a booming revival scene to take the message of the Kingdom to other needy regions

The Father is aware of the Son's love for Him and passion for His work. That is why even before the earthly mission commenced, God had to give a clear word of command to Christ, mandating Him to remain in heaven after His ascension.

King David was prophetically in tune to hear the Father converse with the Son. The words he heard and wrote are significant to us in these last days.

> "The LORD said unto my Lord, *Sit thou* at my right hand, until I make thine enemies thy footstool" (Psalm 110:1 KJV).

The Father had to specifically instruct the Son to *sit* at His right hand after the atonement was accomplished. If this direct "order" was not given, maybe Jesus Christ would have physically come down to earth once every century to motivate His Church to action (like the Theophany manifestations of the Old Testament). Records of Church history hint that Christ would have been prompted to come many times. After all, the Lord longs to take His Bride, the Church, to the place where He is (John 14:1-3).

The Father's word to the Lord Jesus, "sit down", has kept the Son in heaven till now. Thank God for Christ's obedience to the command of the Father (the same way He was obedient unto death during His earthly existence). However, this does not, in any way, reduce Christ's passion and zeal for the Father's work.

WHEN WILL CHRIST STAND UP FROM HIS THRONE?

Jesus Christ obeyed the word of the Father to sit in heaven, but it is certain that He will not sit there forever. Of course, He is forever enthroned King of kings and Lord of lords, but He will one day literally stand up from His throne and come into the earthly realms for the Bride He loves.

We all have this hope that our Saviour will come to take us to the place where He Himself is. He has not only gone to prepare a place for us, but has also promised to come and take us there. This hope is central to our faith. It is the foundation of our preaching. It is our motivation for righteous living. Paul wrote, "If only for this life we have hope in Christ, we are to be pitied more than all men" (see 1 Corinthians 15:12-19).

The question now is *when will Jesus come to take us home?* In other words, *when will Jesus stand up from His throne and appear in the clouds according to the testimony of Scripture?*

The answer can be found in the words that King David heard in the spirit.

> "The LORD said unto my Lord, Sit thou at my right hand, *until I make thine enemies thy footstool*" (Psalm 110:1 KJV *emphasis added*).

The word *until* demarcates Christ's sitting period from His standing period. It indicates the length of time Christ would have to sit at the right hand of God. In other words, *after* the enemies of Christ have been fully subdued, then and only then, can He rise up from the throne to fetch His Bride, the Church. If the enemies of Christ are not fully subdued, then He will have to remain seated in heaven.

This is a simple and logical conclusion based on the text we are considering. Notwithstanding, we can raise another question from this assertion: *Are the enemies of Christ not already in subjection under His feet?* The answer: Yes and No.

We are the "Body of Christ" today. He is *our* Head and we are *His* Body. The subduing of Christ's enemies under *His* feet, therefore, means that they are in subjection to the Church - subject to our exercise of Kingdom authority. Which implies that even though "God placed all things under his feet and appointed him to be head over everything for the Church" (Ephesians 1:22), the Church still has to walk in and manifest this authority by claiming every ground possible for the Kingdom of God.

The Bible says, "in putting everything under him (man), God left nothing that is not subject to him. *Yet at present* we do not see everything subject to him" (Hebrews 2:8). This realisation may be the reason why Paul prayed for the Romans, that "the God of peace will soon crush Satan under your feet" (Romans 16:20).

Positionally, we have a subdued enemy, but we need to actualise this dominion *experientially*. We have to exercise this authority in every sector of the world. In parallel contrast, God *promised* Israel the land of Canaan, but they had to *possess* it through warfare. They had to march into every nook and corner of the land before the promise could become a reality (Joshua 1:1-9). The land was theirs as much as they were willing to place their feet on the promised soil and fight every opposition that arose against them. The Church also needs to march into all the world and put the devil where He belongs - under our feet! This includes all the nations that seem to be closed to the gospel today.

CHRONOS AND *KAIROS*

Let us take this question a step further. The coming of Christ will happen at a particular *time* and *season*. Many have sought to work out this *time* by studying apocalyptic scriptures and observing world events, especially developments in the Middle East. People who *lack* understanding scoff, "Where is this 'coming' he promised?" (2 Peter 3:3,4). Those who "have understanding" try to predict the time and date! Christ, however, made it clear that "No one knows about that day or hour, not even the angels in heaven, *nor the Son*, but only the Father" (Matthew 24:36 *emphasis added*). The same Father who commanded the Son to "Sit down" will one day command Him to "Stand up". He will issue the command at a *time* that He "has set by His own authority" (Acts 1:7). This is why the Son does not know the exact moment.

Every attempt to predict the date of Christ's coming, therefore, is ridiculous. People who dabble into this mystery do not understand that God does not measure time the way we do. We measure time *chronologically* - in years, months, weeks, days, hours, minutes and seconds. God does not. He measures time *prophetically* and *conditionally*. In other words, it is only after certain conditions are fulfilled that the due time for subsequent prophetic events can come. World events may, indeed, give an indication of the *season* of Christ's coming, but they cannot give adequate information about the *date*.

These different perspectives are evident in two particular Greek words that translate into the word "time". *Chronos* pertains to a space of time, while *kairos* pertains to specific events that are *due* at the time. *Chronos* marks quantity while *kairos* marks quality. We live in *chronos* and God works in *kairos*.

The realisation of prophecies will sometimes exceed *our* perceived timing (*chronos*) because prophecies do not come to pass until their *kairos* conditions are met. The exact time for Christ's coming, itself a major prophetic event, will, therefore, not mature in minutes and seconds (*chronos*) but in the progressive fulfilment of conditions effected by forceful men and women who understand the due time (*kairos*). By people "of Issachar, who [understand] the *times* and [know] what [the Church] should do" (1 Chronicles 12:32).

God "hath *in due times* manifested his word" (Titus 1:3 KJV). The reappearance of our Lord will come to pass in *its* time - and God "has made everything beautiful in *its* time" (Ecclesiastes 3:11

emphasis added). Truly, God's ways are not our ways.
Time in the spiritual realm is different from time in
the physical realm. "One day is with the Lord as a
thousand years, and a thousand years as one day" (2
Peter 3:8 KJV).

**The exact time for Christ's
coming, itself a major
prophetic event, will, therefore,
not mature in minutes and
seconds (*chronos*) but in the
progressive fulfilment of
conditions effected by forceful
men and women who under-
stand the due time (*kairos*).**

UNTIL THEN AND NOT BEFORE

What is the significance of all the above to us
here on earth and to our Saviour who is in heaven?

Simply put, Jesus Christ will remain seated in
heaven *until* some specific conditions are met. The
revelation of David that we are considering
revealed one of these *untils* (discussed earlier).

> "The LORD said unto my Lord, Sit thou
> at my right hand, *until I make thine
> enemies thy footstool*" (Psalm 110:1 KJV
> *emphasis added*).

Without delving into the interpretation of apocalyptic symbols, figures and dates, and overlooking the pre-mid-post-millennium debates, other *untils* that point to the coming of Jesus Christ will include the following:

Romans 11:25	The fullness of the gentiles must come into the Church.
Luke 21:24	The times of the gentiles must be fulfilled.
Matthew 24:14	The gospel of the kingdom must be preached in the whole world as a witness.
Ephesians 4:13	The body of Christ must attain unity in the faith and in the knowledge of the Son of God.
1 Corinth 11:26	Communion should be celebrated until Christ comes.
Acts 3:21	God must restore all things by "the spirit and power of Elijah" (see Luke 1:17 and Matthew 17:11).

If we crystallise these *kairos* conditions under two headings, in particular, those that fall within our jurisdiction, they would be:

1. Total Restoration

2. World Evangelisation

These, I believe, represent the purpose of God for today, the *kairos* conditions that precede Christ's return. A mature and united Church, walking in the whole measure of the fullness of Christ, must run to the ends of the earth, establishing the

domain of Christ's reign among every tribe, tongue
and nation (Revelation 5:9,10; 7:9,10). The heavens
will hold Christ until all things are restored *in* and
through the Church.

> "Repent, then, and turn to God, so that
> you sins may be wiped out, that times
> of refreshing may come from the Lord,
> and that he may send Christ, who has
> been appointed for you - even Jesus. *He*
> *must remain in heaven until the time comes*
> *for God to restore everything, as promised*
> *long ago through his holy prophets"* (Acts
> 3:19-21 *emphasis added*).

The following statement sums up the *kairos*
conditions that determine when Christ will come
for His saints:

> The Church will not 'go up' *until* she
> has 'grown up' (Dr. Bill Hamon, *empha-*
> *sis added*).

When the Church *grows up* and *goes out*, Jesus the
Christ will certainly *come down*.

IN AND *THROUGH* THE CHURCH

God is determined to restore the Church to
fullness. The Spirit of revelation is exploding in the
hearts of His people, bringing the whole counsel of
God to life. It will take a restored Church to restore
the world. Authority, purity, unity and the destiny
of the Church must be restored before Christ

comes. The Church, in turn, will move strategically to minister restoration and reconciliation to a world that has been subjected to death and decay (Romans 8:20-22). Church, the time is now!

This calls for much wisdom and understanding. It is essential that we fully realise the season for the corporate expression of the Church. Remember that God's original purpose was for a community of people and not just a single couple. This purpose is now being fulfilled in Christ, the firstborn from the dead. Complete restoration, therefore, points to the corporate Christ united "in the faith and in the knowledge of the Son of God" (Ephesians 4:13).

A mature and united Church, walking in the whole measure of the fullness of Christ, must run to the ends of the earth, establishing the domain of Christ's reign among every tribe, tongue and nation.

The Son of God will not appear the second time until the Church subdues *all* the enemies of God and it will take a mature, united expression of the Church to carry this out.

> "[God's] intent was that now, through the Church, the manifold wisdom of God should be made known to the

rulers and authorities in the heavenly
realms, according to his eternal purpose
which he accomplished in Christ Jesus
our Lord" (Ephesians 3:10,11).

This parallels what King David heard in the
Spirit:

"The LORD says to my Lord: 'Sit at my
right hand until I make your enemies a
footstool for your feet (the Church)'.
The LORD will extend your mighty
sceptre from Zion (the Church); you
will rule in the midst of your
enemies" (Psalm 110:1,2).

God's intention is for the Church to extend the
rule of His Kingdom in all the earth. If Jesus Christ
is the King of kings (and He is), then there should
be no limitation to the realm of His authority. His
glory and the knowledge of His majesty should
cover the earth "as the waters cover the
sea" (Habakkuk 2:14). This is God's purpose and
the Church's end-time responsibility.

"Of the increase of [Christ's] government and peace there will be no end.
He will reign on David's throne and
over his kingdom, establishing and
upholding it with justice righteousness
from that time on and for ever. The zeal
of the LORD Almighty will accomplish
it" (Isaiah 9:7).

When Christ's mighty sceptre is extended to all the earth through the Church, the Lord will arise from His glorious throne and receive His triumphant Church unto Himself in style!

The answer to the question, "Why is Christ still sitting in heaven?", is therefore clear:

The Church has not yet attained complete maturity and unity in the faith.

The Church has not finished the work of extending the Lord's rule in all the earth.

The Church is yet to fully minister restoration and reconciliation to the world.

The Church has not yet subdued *all* of Christ's enemies.

As soon as these things are accomplished by the co-operation of the Church with the Holy Spirit, Christ will Himself come to subdue the final enemy of God, which is death.

> "For as in Adam all die, so in Christ all will be made alive. But each in his own turn: Christ, the first fruits; then, when he comes those who belong to him. *Then the end will come* when he hands over the Kingdom to God the Father *after* he has destroyed all dominion, authority and power. *For he must reign until he has put all his enemies under his feet. The last enemy to be destroyed is death"* (1 Corinthians 15:22-26 *emphasis added*).

If we truly desire the appearance of our Saviour Jesus Christ in majesty and glory, then we need to wake up to our end-time responsibility, key into the purpose of God, run into all the earth and finish the work entrusted into our hands.

It is time to run, Church! It is time to run!

> "'Not by might nor by power, but by my Spirit,' says the LORD Almighty" (Zechariah 4:6).

5 | THE GREAT TRANSITION

The ball of human destiny is in the court of the Church! It has been there for the past 2,000 years! Our Lord and King, Jesus Christ, together with the great cloud of heavenly witnesses, continue to watch with keen interest how we will play this "destiny ball". Their attention is now on the end-time Church, today's generation of believers. They consider us the generation with possibly the greatest opportunity to accomplish the divine purpose - a feat that will activate the return of Christ.

Are we going to follow the trend of Church history by revelling in part-victories and work half done? Are we not going to stop playing against ourselves, stop scoring "own goals", and start advancing aggressively towards the gates of the enemy? Is it not time to double up our efforts, focus more squarely on purpose and fill the whole earth with the knowledge of the glory of God? Heaven is watching. Jesus is waiting. Time is ticking away, and so are our opportunities.

THE PLACE OF WILLINGNESS

We are the army of God and we are in a fight. Like Joshua against the allied kings, we need to completely subdue the enemies of God and speed up the coming Christ. Very crucial at this time is the place of willingness in the camp of the Lord.

No army can win a war with soldiers who are unwilling to fight. Not only should the soldiers be willing, *all* the soldiers, with singleness of heart, need to engage in battle. Superior armoury will prove useless if the soldiers refuse to use them. The position of the Church, in the context of completing the purposes of God, is sometimes like the men of Ephraim in the Bible:

> "The men of Ephraim, *though armed with bows, turned back on the day of battle*" (Psalm 78:9 *emphasis added*).

We are armed with more than bows in our generation. We have every kind of Bible under the sun. Our reference materials are just as many as our Bibles. We have teachers who "specialise" on different conference topics (including weight watching!). We are indeed armed for battle, but is it not a mystery that so many turn back on the *day* of battle?

For one reason or the other, when it comes to the battles of the kingdom; when we are expected to unite together to do the works of Jesus and accomplish the purposes of God, many tend to retreat to the safety of their tents. We choose our traditions and resist seasons of transition. We preserve our comfort zones and tolerate the enemy of progress. Our agenda take precedence over the Spirit's agenda.

This generation is best equipped to walk in the fullness of biblical revelation. Everyone in the Body of Christ has the potential to flow in gifts of the Spirit. Why is there such a deviation from God's standards? Why are His purposes lingering? Is it the size of our Goliath or the ignorance of our covenant rights that is keeping us from advancing the will of God? Could it be a shallow understanding of God's divine purposes (see chapters 1-3) or the absence of vision (see chapter 7) that is causing this regressing demeanour? Could it be that the enemy of righteousness has succeeded in draining the motivation of believers through shame and intimidation? Whatever the reason, unwillingness is a liability in the kingdom of God.

THE UNWILLING MAJORITY

There are, indeed, some in the camp of the Lord who are willing to sacrifice their very lives for God's concerns. The problem, however, is that these "some" have always been few. The faithful remnant, those with a sense of purpose and direction, are not always the majority. Only those who know and feel the heartbeat of God yield to the call of God and fight His battles.

When Deborah and Barak went to war against Jabin, a Canaanite king, they met two categories of people in the Lord's camp - the willing and the unwilling. Some, consumed with the zeal of the Lord, made themselves available on the day of battle.

> "Some came from Ephraim, whose roots were in Amalek; Benjamin was with the people who followed. From Makir captains came down, from Zebulun those who bear a commander's staff. The princes of Issachar were with Deborah; yes, Issachar was with Barak, rushing after him into the valley... The people of Zebulun risked their very lives; so did Nephtali on the heights of the field" (Judges 5:14,15a,18).

Even though Israel won the battle through these willing soldiers, Deborah still expressed her disappointment in those who did not bother to involve themselves with the ongoing war.

> "In the districts of Reuben there was much searching of heart (probably, 'Should I go? Should I stay? Should I give? Should I withhold?'). Why did you stay among the campfires to hear the whistling for the flocks? In the districts of Reuben there was much

searching of heart. Gilead stayed beyond the Jordan. And Dan, why did he
linger by the ships (his merchandise)?
Asher remained on the coast and stayed
in his coves (they could not cancel their
holiday reservation!)" (Judges 5:15b-17
additions mine).

What a sharp contrast there is between the willing and the unwilling! A quest for victory against
the Lord's enemies was enough to motivate the
willing warriors to battle (this also meant victory
and peace for their families and the whole nation).
The unwilling fighters, on the other hand, decided
to put their personal affairs and physical conven-
ience before the nation's interest.

**There are, indeed, some in
the camp of the Lord who are
willing to sacrifice their very
lives for God's concerns. The
problem, however, is that these
"some" have always been few.**

We all need to ask ourselves some pertinent
questions that could affect our destiny in God's
kingdom: On which side am I stationed? The *fighting* or the *retreating* side? Am I willing to fight the
Lord's battles or prone to drawing back on the day
of battle? Am I running with God's vision for my
life or pursuing my own selfish dreams?

In this matter, every man must answer for himself.
However, there is a serious statement in Deborah's
song that probably reveals the heart of God towards
unwilling fighters. Could this be His verdict against
any generation of unwilling believers?

> "'Curse Meroz', said the angel of the
> LORD. 'Curse its people bitterly, be-
> cause they did not come to help the
> LORD, to help the LORD against the
> mighty'" (Judges 5:23).

Prophet Amos also spoke out God's heart along
these same lines:

> "Woe to you who are complacent in
> Zion, and to you who feel secure on
> Mount Samaria" (Amos 6:1).

Jesus Christ, in the New Testament, gave His
specific verdict on lukewarm believers (people who
are useless for advancing heaven's purpose):

> "I know your deeds, that you are
> neither cold not hot. I wish you were
> either one or the other! So, because you
> are lukewarm - neither hot nor cold - I
> am about to spit you out of my
> mouth" (Revelation 3:15,16).

Once again, which side are you on, the *willing* or
the *unwilling*?

EVERYONE IS NEEDED IN BATTLE

Even though God can (and does) win His battles through a few, He still desires everyone to be willing and courageous enough to engage in warfare for the Kingdom. Moses once expressed this thought when he wished that *"all* the LORD'S people were prophets and that the LORD would put his Spirit on them!" (Numbers 11:29). God will not turn back anyone who enlists Himself for the Master's use. The problem is that the majority are unwilling to fight spiritual warfare in the ends of the earth and only a few are concerned about the concerns of God. We are now used to seeing and applauding one 'superstar' perform spiritual exploits, forgetting that we are called to be participators and not spectators. Is it not easy to comprehend, therefore, that God, the first on the list of purpose-driven ones, will sometimes take violent action to fulfil His purpose?

In our time, as in past times, the Lord will react to our attitude to His work. He will once again intervene for the sake of His purpose. He needs everyone's hand on the plough, doing everything necessary for the accomplishment of His purposes in the earth. Jesus Himself expressed this thought when He observed the amount of work that remained undone on the harvest field:

> "When he saw the crowds, he had compassion on them, because they were harassed and helpless, like sheep without a shepherd. Then he said to his

> disciples, 'The harvest is plentiful *but
> the workers are few*. Ask the Lord of the
> harvest, therefore, to send out *[more]
> workers* into his harvest field" (Matthew
> 9:36-38; *emphasis added*).

God's intervention at this time would result in the thrusting forth of more labourers into the harvest field. The prophecy of David that we have been considering reveals this intention of God.

> "The LORD says to my Lord: 'Sit at my
> right hand until I make your enemies a
> footstool for your feet'. The LORD will
> extend your mighty sceptre from Zion;
> you will rule in the midst of your
> enemies. *Your troops will be willing on
> your day of battle.* Arrayed in holy
> majesty, from the womb of the dawn
> you will receive the dew of your
> youth" (Psalm 110:1-3 *emphasis added*).

In the King James Version of the Bible, the first part of the 3rd verse reads: *Thy people shall be willing in the day of thy power.* Who are God's people? You and I. Everyone in the Body of Christ. We all, in the context of subduing all the enemies of Christ, will be willing (or be made willing) in the day of God's power.

Other versions of this verse say:

> "Your people will offer themselves will-
> ingly in the day of Your power" (Amp).

"Thy people will volunteer freely in the day of thy power" (NASB).

"In that day of your power, your people shall come to you willingly" (LB).

"On the day you fight your enemies, your people will volunteer" (GNB).

The truth is that God needs everyone on the battle-field. Everyone is expected to contribute to the extension of the rule of Christ. God will ensure that this happens in the day of His power.

REVIVAL DAYS!

Now, when is the *day* of God's power? In which day, according to David's revelation, will we witness an explosion of willingness in the camp of the Lord?

It could be no other day than the day when God revives His people and His work. It is the day when God graciously sends His Spirit to refresh His troops. It is the time when God, through His choice servants, intervenes in the course of Church History and turns the hearts of His people to Himself again.

Everyone is expected to contribute to the extension of the rule of Christ.

Looking back, we can point to many of such "days", times of revival that resulted in an unprecedented extension in the rule of Christ. If it were not for revival, the Church probably would have lost extensive grounds to the archenemy of God.

Revival is what we are "expecting" today, the day of God's power that recommits people to their Maker. There is evidence from past revivals that God's purpose is advanced at such times. The hearts of sinful men are turned to God. Many believers become willing vessels of honour. More warriors of righteousness are enlisted and impacted with strength to run to the battle lines. In short, many are enabled to make a transition from unwillingness to willingness. There is, no doubt, an urgent need for the Lord to revive His work again for a speedy execution of the divine mandate.

If there is anything we should pray and cry out to God for, it should be a genuine revival in the Church and world. A move of God's Spirit that would wake up the sleeping giant called the Church. A revival of genuine oneness in Christ. We need an urgent arousing today that will advance God's purpose on the earth.

Revival wakes up the Church when she sleeps.

Revival shakes up the Church when she slumbers.

Revival quickens the Church when she slacks.

Revival refocuses the Church when she is disoriented.

Revival heats up the Church when she is cold.

Revival speeds up the Church when she is sluggish.

We need the final move of God at this time, a violent outpouring of the Spirit of God that will revive every dry bone and turn every valley of complacency into a mountain of everlasting burning. Now is the day of God's power; the time of His refreshing.

> "For it is God who works in you (corporately speaking, especially during revival days!) to will and to act according to his good purpose" (Philippians 2:13 addition mine).

VOLUNTEERS AND LABOURERS

Revivals are not only times of refreshing, but also times for work! A revival is not an end in itself. Every past revival had its purpose. God used them not only to save the lost and quicken the saved, but also to restore a variety of spiritual truth that got lost during the "dark ages". The final revival will also have its purpose.

God will send us revival today not just to bless us and make us happy, but specifically to prepare us for the second coming of Jesus Christ. He will bring us to a place of conformity to every written counsel in the Bible. He will restore holiness and zeal in the Church. He will stir us up and unlock our willingness to be part of His advancing army. The purpose of the final revival includes the release of volunteers and labourers into the harvest field for the completion of the Church's mandate; for the salvation of the last batch of gentiles that must enter the Kingdom (Romans 11:25).

I *still* believe in revival! I am persuaded that a great outpouring of God is yet to come upon the earth. I cannot stop writing about what I have heard from the Lord. Concerning the move of God that is underway, I once wrote the following:

> Every revival since the time of Martin Luther, essentially, has been the manifestation of God's glory through *a person* (or at best, a group of people). The main purpose of these revivals (up until now) was *the restoration of eroded truths and the harvesting of lost souls living in those generations.* The final revival will have a unique purpose distinct from all the others. It will be a display of glory through *all* of God's people *as we walk in all the restored truths of God and engage in the greatest and final ingathering of souls before the coming of Jesus Christ.* (*Ultimate Destiny,* pp 107,108 *emphasis added*).

Every revival in these last days that does not result in the release of labourers into the harvest field is not fulfilling its ultimate mandate. It is one thing to cry at God's altar, it is a different thing to receive fresh fire from the altar and go with zeal to serve the God of the altar. The final revival will cause the army of God to rise in power and reflect the glory of God in all the earth.

WILLING AND OBEDIENT

As God restores the revelation of His word and purpose to fullness in the Church, we would be faced with the challenge to obey. For full blessing, willingness must be coupled with obedience.

> "If you are willing *and* obedient, you will eat the best from the land" (Isaiah 1:19 *emphasis added*).

It seems we have chosen to give our allegiance to sections of God's word that make us comfortable. This is reflected in our choice of speakers and Bible expositors. Is this not a characteristic of the last days, a time "when men will not put up with sound doctrine" (2 Timothy 4:3)? If we would be counted among the willing, we cannot afford to have itchy ears for selected truth. We must open our hearts and receive all that God wants to teach and reveal to us - especially through His apostles and prophets.

Revivals are not only times of refreshing, but also times for work!

Truth about unity in the Church is available today; we must be willing and obedient.

Truth about the reconciliation of corporate conflicts is available today; we must be willing and obedient.

Truth about the expected lifestyle and conduct of believers is available today; we must be willing and obedient.

Truth about the need for and practice of powerful intercessory prayer is available today; we must be willing and obedient.

Truth about our mandate to reach the ends of the earth before Christ comes is available today; we must be willing and obedient.

Communicators of truth should no more satisfy themselves with a mere show of willingness in the believers (the crowd that come to hear the word or the applause that appends catchphrases), but must travail (inwardly desire and intensely pray) for the full formation of Christ in their hearts. This was Paul's burden during his ministry (Galatians 4:19). He did not want the faith of his hearers to rest on men's wisdom but on the power of God (1 Corinthians 2:4,5). This is also the purpose of God in this day of His power.

THE JOY OF REVIVAL

As willingness and obedience explodes in the Church, all heaven will rejoice! Our lives will bring much praise to God! The salvation of sinners, the subduing of the nations, the building of the Church, the fulfilment of God's counsels, all these will produce waves of joy in the Kingdom of God!

> "Will you not revive us again, that your
> people may rejoice in you?" (Psalm 85:6).

After Deborah and the willing soldiers in Israel subdued the Canaanites, the whole camp broke out in spontaneous singing.

> "When the princes in Israel take the lead, when the people willingly offer themselves - praise the LORD!... My heart is with Israel's princes, *with the willing volunteers among the people.* Praise the LORD! So may all your enemies perish, O Lord! But may they who love you be like the sun when it rises in its strength" (Judges 5:2,9,31 *emphasis added*).

May you and I be among those who bring joy to the camp of the Lord! The whole of heaven rejoices when a sinner repents. Jesus Christ gives a standing ovation when God's purpose advances. Yielding oneself to God as a good soldier pleases our Commanding Officer. We are entering an endless season of joy in the House of God because these are the days of His power!

6 | THE NIGHT IS PREGNANT!

It is obvious that God is up to something in our day and time. He is all out for the fulfilment of His divine plan through the Church. This is why He will visit us once again with unprecedented revival.

In order for us to experience a revival that will advance God's purposes significantly, God must raise up revivalists and reformers in the Church. These are men and women with fire in their bones. People aflame with holy zeal. Apostles and prophets who have the *now* word of the Lord in their mouth. Believers who have felt the heartbeat of God. Forceful people who will not love their lives even in the face of death. We desperately need more people aflame in our generation of destiny.

The move of God is in fact the move of His people, for God must find willing vessels through which He can perform His righteous acts. When God lays hold of a man, the man lays hold of the Kingdom. Just like Paul, the Apostle to the Gentiles, the resolution of God's man or woman is, "I press on to take hold of that for which Christ Jesus took hold of me" (Philippians 3:12). With such a determination in a yielded believer, God can accomplish great things according to His predetermined counsel.

God does not use only a portion of man. He uses every dimension of his existence. The person upon whom God lays His hand would have no choice but to surrender everything for God's use. Desires will turn around completely. Motivations would come from above and from within. Strength would be spent for the cause of God's Kingdom and His righteousness. The life of such a person would be totally devoted to God.

Can you be counted as one of God's consecrated servants in these last days of His power? Can God use you to prepare the way for the coming of Christ? Do not be in doubt. God has you in mind. The revelation of King David hints that God is going to release the willingness of His *troops* and not just a few saints. If you have the strength to serve God, chances are He is already preparing you for battle!

"FROM THE WOMB OF THE DAWN"

As the prophecy of David continues to reveal, many of the people that God will lay hold upon in these last days of His power will be those who have been prepared through the fires of affliction. They will be people who have had a first-hand revelation of God during their "darkest hour of the night". Through them, God will revive His work and close this age of grace. He will place in them a divine sense of purpose and urgency. Let us consider David's revelation again and establish this from the word of God.

> "The LORD says to my Lord: 'Sit at my right hand until I make your enemies a footstool for you feet'. The LORD will extend your mighty sceptre from Zion; you will rule in the midst of your enemies. Your troops will be willing on you day of battle. Arrayed in holy majesty, *from the womb of the dawn* you will receive the dew of your youth" (Psalm 110:1-3 *emphasis added*).

The dawn signifies a new day, the appearance of light after protracted darkness. It refers to a breakthrough after a period of gloom; joy after much weeping. The truth is, many have had to endure much affliction in the wilderness seasons of life.

While others seemed to be moving ahead, they have found themselves confined to "the cave of Adullam". Like David, they are anointed but not yet appointed! They are conscious of the covenant promises of God, but confessing them sometimes brought confusion instead of possession! Frustrated by their waiting season, they have moaned, "I have laboured to no purpose; I have spent my strength in vain and for nothing" (Isaiah 49:4a).

God has used wilderness seasons to try some of His people. He has used hard times to chastise others. Some have been in oblivion receiving the word of the Lord. Others have been learning to depend on God *alone*. The night is now heavy with child! The dawn is about to break! God's troops are coming forth from the four corners of the earth!

Have you been going through difficult times lately? Do not despair, a new day is in view! When you cross over to "the other side" you would have much comfort to give to others who are going through similar circumstances. It takes a restored person to be a restorer of bruised people.

A strong revival is building from the grassroots. It will break out through the lives and witness of those who have experienced first-hand, personal transformation. God's troops are coming forth with the full revelation of God's counsels in their heart. The mysteries of the Kingdom are unveiled in their understanding. The power of the Spirit is at work in them. They know their position *in* Christ. The love of God is shed abroad amongst them. Through these ones, new things cometh!

The valley of dry bones may represent "darkness" but revival is the joy that comes in the morning (see Isaiah 9:2,3; Psalm 126:5,6). The final day of God's power is dawning upon us (Dr. Bill Hamon calls it *The Day of the Saints*).   It is here already. In many places in the Body of Christ, the morning has dawned. In other places, the darkness is coming to an end. Look up and behold, it's a new day! The night is going to produce its young!

It takes a restored person to be a restorer of bruised people.

YOUNG MEN LIKE THE DEW

Let us notice something important that will happen at this break of dawn:

> "Your troops will be willing on your day of battle. Arrayed in holy majesty, from the womb of the dawn *you will receive the dew of your youth*" (Psalm 110:3 *emphasis added*).

As the dawn breaks in the Church, it is interesting to note that many of those who will emerge as revival carriers will be *young men* (used in a generic sense to include women). These will come to God "like the dew" (see margin of the NIV Bible). In other words, one of the fruits of wilderness dealings will be the raising up of many young people enthused with the mandate to extend the Kingdom of God. They will surrender totally to the One who has called them. They shall run with speed in obedience to their Lord's command.

Notice also that these young men and women will not just arise, but they will come forth in their numbers. They will fill the earth with the glory of God - just as the dew from heaven leaves no spot on the earth untouched when it falls. Men and women from every nation will boldly proclaim the goodness of the Lord in these last days.

Ezekiel did not see a few soldiers after the dry-bone revival. Instead, he witnessed the uprising of a "vast number" of them (Ezekiel 37:10). The mighty men of valour that made themselves available for King David (a type of Christ) when he was on his way to the throne of Israel did not come in twos or threes either, but in great numbers until they were comparable with the army of God.

> "Day after day men came to help David, *until he had a great army, like the army of God*" (1 Chronicles 12:22 *emphasis added*).

Particularly, they came to David with a single purpose:

> "All these were fighting men *who volunteered to serve in the ranks. They came to Hebron fully determined to make David king over all Israel.* All the rest of the Israelites were also of one mind to make David king" (1 Chronicles 12:28 *emphasis added*).

Oh, that we all will fully determine to make Jesus Christ King over all the principalities, powers and dominions of the world! He is King, no doubt, but we need to possess the nations for Him. Every believer should partake in this. We all need to volunteer ourselves in God's army, not just a handful of us, but everyone - like the falling of the sweet morning dew! According to the context of David's revelation, this will come to pass as a result of the final revival and the explosion of willingness in God's people.

WHY YOUNG MEN?

Why does the Bible specifically mention "young men" as the fighting force during the days of God's battle? Simply: because young people have the strength to *run* about for the extension of the Kingdom of God. (We can also interpret the usage of the phrase "young men" in David's revelation to mean the "young" offspring of the night (*wilderness seasons*); the innovation, creativity and freshness of ideas that will come from those who have taken time to know the voice of the Holy Spirit). Young people, generally, have the strength and mental alertness that is needed on the battle field.

> "The glory of young men is their strength" (Proverbs 20:29).

> "I write to you, young men, because you are strong, and the word of God

lives in you, and you have overcome
the evil one" (1 John 2:14).

Commanding officers do not recruit old, worn-
out grandfathers to fight in the warfront. The
Greatest Man of War will not do it either. God will
mobilise both spiritually and physically fit people,
"all those... who are *able* to serve in the
army" (Numbers 26:2).

While it is true that the majority of these mobilised warriors will be young, please understand
that God's usage of the word "youth" can exclude
some physically young people like the sons of Eli
(1 Samuel 2:12) and include some physically old
people like Caleb (Joshua 14:10-12).

The advancement of purpose requires strength,
energy, swiftness and spiritual agility. God will
supply spiritual strength, but nonetheless, physical
stamina will be required. The physically weak,
especially people given to idleness and slothful-
ness, cannot advance God's Kingdom. God does
not anoint laziness. He calls and anoints strong,
hard-working people. The strength of the youth is
an asset to God in the days of His power.

We have a duty to be good stewards over our
physical bodies. Exercising the muscles, eating
healthily, resting adequately are all profitable
activities we should not neglect.

If the Church will finish the mandate of God in
this generation, then Church leaders should
consider their young people as assets and not
liabilities; contributors and not competitors.

God is calling the young. He is giving them visions of a preferable future (see chapter 7). Leaders need to tap into their resourcefulness and creativity and channel their strength towards fruitful service. The experience of the old and the exuberance of the young should operate side-by-side in these last days of God's power.

THE WISDOM OF THE OLD

If strength is the glory of young men, "grey hair [is] the splendour of the old" (Proverbs 22:29). Grey hair signifies wisdom gained from experience. Young men may have zeal, but the old can add the knowledge dimension usually missing in zeal. It is important at this time for both young and old to work together in accomplishing the purposes of God.

The advancement of purpose requires strength, energy, swiftness and spiritual agility.

Certainly, the final revival will produce young warriors, but they would not look down on older ministers. We have endured a time when the "old" and the "young" exclude each other. A new day has dawned! We need one another. The final revival will restore the function of apostolic fathers in the Church and true mentors will once again guide the young. The strength of the youth and the wisdom of the old must combine to deal a final deathblow against the devil.

God has an agenda to reconcile the young with the old and the old with the young. Our hearts must be turned towards each other if there is going to be progress in the Kingdom (Malachi 4:5,6). We must run together and complete the counsels of God. (For more wisdom on the reconciliation of generational conflict, see my book *Ultimate Destiny*, *pages 95-104*).

ELEVENTH HOUR MISSIONARIES

Many people, fresh from their individual seasons of trial, are crying out for God to use them. They desire to work for God in this final hour and want to implement the dreams in their hearts. However, there seems to be a crucial problem. Many in leadership are sacrificing the strength of the young on the altar of personal interest.

> "About the eleventh hour he went out and found still others standing around. He asked them, 'Why have you been standing here all day long doing nothing?' *'Because no-one has hired us,'* *they answered.* He said to them, 'You also go and work in my vineyard'" (Matthew 20:7,8 *emphasis added*).

Are we sensitive to the heart cry of the people emerging from the shadows of the night? Who will take the risk of utilising the zeal and creativity that they possess to advance the Kingdom of God? In this eleventh hour of destiny, Church leaders should mobilise every willing-but-presently-idle believer for active Kingdom service.

Kingdom resources (young people in particular) are being under-utilised and misappropriated today. It is not enough for thousands of able-bodied believers to gather in a church assembly to promote the ministry of one person. The purpose of the five-fold ministry of Christ in the church is to equip the believers and release them for the work of the ministry. Nowadays, we see the believers gather every week to "release" the five-fold ministry of Christ!

The final revival will restore the function of apostolic fathers in the Church and true mentors will once again guide the young.

The question is this: Are the believers duly employed in the Lord's vineyard? Is the emphasis on what God wants to do in and through *them* or on what is being done through the *"man of God"*? Both local and global missions need an infusion of more labourers and God's people must be mobilised and released to do the work.

For instance, with the view of completing the task of reaching every ethnic group in the world, George Verwer made a breakdown of the number of missionaries the Church in each nation has to send - called the *Acts 13 Breakthrough* (*Out of the Comfort Zone*, pg.). These numbers need to be mobilised, trained, sent and supported. The 40/70 window, which includes the continent of Europe right through to Northern India and Japan, is being targeted by missiologists and prayer strategists as, probably, the final harvest frontier of the world. These regions need *troops* of workers, weeks of intercession and millions of pounds.

Indeed, opportunities abound for people to be involved in the Lord's work. In fact, the "mission field" of the 21st century (the eleventh hour) has changed. God is raising "missionaries" in the workplace, saints who will not confine the glory of God to the four walls of a church service. The supernatural power of God will manifest on the streets and in homes. No one should remain unemployed" in these final days. The word of the Lord to everyone is, "Go and work in my vineyard." (For a fuller discussion on this unique feature of God's last day move, see chapters 7 and 8 of *The Day of the Saints*).

THOSE WHO WAIT UPON THE LORD

Thank God for the strength of the young! Thank God for the wisdom of the old! Thank God for seasons of personal affliction that give birth to a desire to be used of God! If there is only one lesson to be learnt in the wilderness, it must be that physical strength is not sufficient to do the will of God.

Many try to run the divine race in their own strength. Others employ human wisdom in the ministry. No wonder why there are reports of burnout and breakdowns in the ranks of the Lord's army. No wonder why there is powerlessness in the pulpit and purposelessness in the pew!

Even young people with obvious calls of God upon their lives, lack inner drive because of one failure or the other. Many avoid spiritual warfare or involvement in ministry for fear of getting hurt again. Avoiding the divine mandate is not the solution. What is necessary is to regain lost strength and recapture blurred vision. God is a God of recovery and restoration.

Those who come to God, fully depending upon His grace, will experience a renewal of strength and a refreshing from the presence of the Lord.

> "He gives strength to the weary and increases the power of the weak. Even youths grow tired and weary, and young men stumble and fall; *but those who hope in the LORD (wait upon the Lord - KJV) will renew their strength.* They will soar on wings like eagles; they will run and not grow weary, they will walk and not be faint" (Isaiah 40:29-31 *emphasis added*).

If there is any time for the Church to wait on God, it is now. Both young and old need God's grace and strength. The journey is still long and the time short. Only the ever-available strength of God, the anointing of His Spirit, can empower us to complete the unfinished work.

Let us return to the Lord for strength at this time because nothing can substitute for the divine infusion of God's power. The early disciples were told specifically to wait in Jerusalem until they were endued with power from on high. We also have to wait on the Lord. Only with the power of the Holy Spirit can we go into all the earth "doing good and healing [all] who are under the power of the devil" (Acts 10:38).

HOLY MAJESTY

Let us remember that God is out to fulfil His divine purpose through the Church and thereafter send Jesus Christ to take His Bride into glory. With this in mind, it is easy to comprehend the priority of holiness in the Lord's camp.

Our private and public lives must conform to God's standards because He is clothing His army with majestic robes of holiness.

The warriors that the final revival will produce will not just be young and strong, but also holy and blameless. As David's revelation reveals, they will be "arrayed in holy majesty" (Psalm 110:3). As they go from battle to battle, they will proclaim the holiness of the Lord. They will seek not just the advance of the Kingdom of God, but also the establishment of His righteousness in the earth (Matthew 6:33). The Lord's holiness will make them shine forth in majesty.

The sons of Eli, though young, were useless to God because of their lifestyle of iniquity. Do you desire for God to use you in these last days? Holiness and integrity must be your watchword.

> "Nevertheless, God's solid foundation stands firm, sealed with this inscription: 'The Lord knows those who are his,' and, *'Everyone who confesses the name of the Lord must turn away from wickedness'.* In a large house there are articles not only of gold and silver, but also of wood and clay; some are for noble purposes and some for ignoble. *If a man cleanses himself from the latter, he will be an instrument for noble purposes, made holy, useful to the Master and prepared to do any good work.* Flee the evil desire of youth, and pursue righteousness, faith, love and peace, along with those who call on the Lord out of a pure heart" (2 Timothy 2:19-22 *emphasis added*).

Christ is coming for "a radiant Church, without stain or wrinkle or any other blemish, but *holy and blameless*" (Ephesians 5:27 *emphasis added*). He is going to present His Bride to God dressed in white, which is a sign of purity. Any other state will not gain admittance into the presence of God because "without holiness no one will see the Lord" (Hebrews 12:14).

Holiness is a must in these crucial times. The atrocities committed by those who bear the vessels of God will no more be tolerated. Our private and public lives must conform to God's standards because He is clothing His army with majestic robes of holiness.

There is no time to play around anymore. God has His purpose in view. In one final wave of His mighty right hand, He will restore all things *in* His Church and *through* His Church. He will possess every land that does not yet have the Banner of Christ's rule. He will give the word for Christ to come for the redeemed. May you and I live to see this holy and fearful move of God, and be used of Him in the day of His power.

7 | HOW FAR CAN YOU SEE?

When there is no defined purpose, strength will be abused. Purpose generates vision and a clear sense of direction. Vision born out of purpose will demand the use of strength in a concentrated manner.

The difference, sometimes, between a strong and a weak person is *focus*. Some who seem to be weak may actually possess more inherent strength than they are willing to acknowledge. When someone spreads his strength thinly in many directions, he would no doubt feel weakness compared to someone who concentrates all he has on one task. Maximising the use of strength through focus is wisdom.

In the day of God's power when the Holy Spirit falls afresh upon both young and old, not only will strength be renewed *for* the race, visions *of* the finish line will also be birthed. The Bible says, "it shall come to pass afterwards, that I will pour out my Spirit upon all flesh... *your young men shall see visions*" (Joel 2:28 *emphasis added*). These visions will generate momentum in the recipients and optimise the strength they possess.

GOD'S SECRET WEAPON

God is "the only wise God". He is a God of strategy and objectivity. He fights His battles with great demonstrations of wisdom. Referring to the execution of the redemption plan, Paul gave credit to the secret wisdom of God.

> "We do, however, speak a message of wisdom among the mature, but not the wisdom of this age or of the rulers of this age, who are coming to nothing. No, *we speak of God's secret wisdom*, a wisdom that has been hidden and that God destined for our glory before time began. None of the rulers of this age understood it, for if they had, they would not have crucified the Lord of glory." (1 Corinthians 2:6-8 *emphasis added*).

God declared His plan to redeem man in Eden - with the devil's full attention. The old serpent, hearing this verdict, embarked on a ruthless campaign to eliminate anyone who showed signs of being "the seed of the woman." Barely a chapter after man was driven out of the garden, he instigated Cain against Abel. He then tried to kill Joseph through the envy of his brothers. He went all out to stop the emergence of Moses. He killed many of the prophets of Israel. He caused weeping and great mourning in "Bethlehem and its vicinity" as he sought to assassinate the baby Jesus.

What Satan did not know was that God had a specific season in mind for the fulfilment of the prophetic word. The means of fulfilment was also specific. Such is the wisdom displayed in God's execution of vision.

While the devil was busy exerting his strength, killing people blindly, God's vision of what He wanted to accomplish remained unclouded. Certainly, "Wisdom is better than strength... Wisdom is better than weapons of war" (Ecclesiastes 9:16a, 18a).

> "A wise man attacks the city of the mighty and pulls down the stronghold in which they trust" (Proverbs 21:22).

> "Wisdom makes one wise man more powerful that ten rulers in a city" (Ecclesiastes 7:19).

THE WISDOM OF VISION

The Church is at war (1 Timothy 1:18; Revelation 12:7-9,17) and it is going to take more than strength to win. We have to follow God's example of wisdom.

The impartation and execution of vision by the Spirit of God is a major display of wisdom for achieving complete victory in this war. If we are going to finish the work at hand, we need to rediscover the place of vision in warfare (the importance of vision in the consummation of God's eternal purposes). The extent to which we accomplish God's end-time purposes will depend on how far we perceive our role in it.

> "Where there is no vision (revelation, prophecy, *rhema*), the people perish" (Proverbs 29:18 KJV addition mine).

We need to understand and grasp vision from God's point of view. Without it we cannot run the end-time race. Ministers of the gospel need to give the greater heed because God has entrusted them with the most valuable resource on the battlefield: *people*, God's primary provision for any vision. Money is secondary on the list of vision-necessities, because God does not anoint money; He anoints people. If vision for ministry is absent, then the people involved with the ministry will "cast off restraint" and run off in different directions. As it was in the days of the Judges, everyone will do that which "is right in his own eyes" (Judges 17:6).

It is God who assigns tasks to His servants, specific mandates that accomplish specific portions of the divine plan. He gave Peter a *specific* vision to reach the Jews and Paul a *specific* vision to reach the gentiles (Galatians 2:8). This ensured a maximisation of the potentials of both men and reduced unnecessary duplication of ministry. No wonder then, why the gospel spread *as far* as it did and *as fast* as it did in the days of the Apostles - every aspect of society was covered by specific mandates.

If we are going to finish the work at hand, we need to rediscover the place of vision in warfare (the importance of vision in the consummation of God's purposes).

The absence of Christ-centred vision in the Church is tragic. It results, ultimately, in the underutilisation of our resources and a waste of valuable time. It produces a lot of activity but not total accomplishment. Vision is, therefore, paramount both on a corporate and an individual level.

The emerging young warriors especially need this understanding and depth of insight in order to run precisely and effectively. Subsequent sections of this chapter will give further insight into different aspects of vision as it relates to the work of God's kingdom.

PRIMARY AND SECONDARY FOCUS

Primarily, our focus in the Christian life is on God and His Kingdom. Christ had taught us to "seek first his kingdom and his righteousness" (Matthew 6:33). This entails our walk with *God* **and** our walk with His *people*. As we walk with God, His character and the image of His Son develops *in* us; as we walk with God's people, His love and the life of His Spirit is expressed *through* us. Our calling, therefore, is both personal and corporate. John emphasised this truth when he wrote that our personal walk with God is not complete without a corporate walk with God's people.

> "We love because he first loved us. If anyone says, 'I love God,' yet hates his brother, he is a liar. *For anyone who does not love his brother, whom he has seen, cannot love God, whom he has not seen.* And he has given us this command: Whoever loves God must also love his brother" (1 John 4:19-21 *emphasis added*).

The evil of disunity is that it impedes our walk and weakens our witness. It undercuts the power of God and hinders the world from knowing the manifest glory of Christ. If we will make our calling and election sure, attention must be given to loving God and loving the brotherhood.

Out of this primary focus comes a secondary focal point, namely, God's calling upon and vision for our individual lives *and how this connects with the rest of the Body*. While God maintains a singular purpose and a singular kingdom ("There is *one* body and *one* Spirit - just as you were called to *one* hope when you were called - *one* Lord, *one* faith, *one* baptism; *one* God and Father of all, who is over all and through all and in all" Ephesians 4:4-6), in His wisdom, He gives us all different tasks to fulfil for His glory. Geographically, strategically, technically and in many other ways, our tasks will differ. Hence, this secondary area of focus for people called of God is the individual tasks assigned to each person - a focus that must not be detrimental to the singular purpose of God and the corporate expression of the Church.

> "What, after all, is Apollos? And what is Paul? Only servants, through whom you came to believe - *as the Lord has assigned to each his task*. I planted the seed, Apollos watered it, but God made it grow. So neither he who plants nor he who waters is anything, but only God, who makes things grow. The man who plants and the man who waters have *one purpose*, and each will be rewarded according to his *own labour*" (1 Corinthians 3:5-8 *emphasis added*).

Visions may differ, but purpose will always remain the same - to glorify God. Without God's blessing, individual tasks will not fulfil any purpose; and if anything is achieved, it will not be *His* purpose. If we truly walk with God and love the brotherhood of believers, we will celebrate diversity in the spirit of unity; we will cease from fighting each other and consider ourselves fellow-workers and co-labourers. Both the primary and secondary focus of vision go hand in hand.

The evil of disunity is that it impedes our walk and weakens our witness.

Focusing on our individual callings (secondary focus) without a commitment to the love-walk (primary focus) has allowed for many self-inflicted casualties in the ranks. We need not fight one another if we are in love with each other and, supposedly, are fighting for the same cause. When we work against each other, there is no way of fulfilling the divine purpose.

> "Every kingdom divided against itself *will be ruined,* and every city or household divided against itself *will not stand*" (Matthew 12:25 *emphasis added*).

A VISION FOR COMPLETION

Recalling the *kairos* conditions necessary for the coming of Christ (discussed in chapter 4), it is obvious that God wants to impress a vision for completing His purposes upon His people. Broadly speaking, this will come in two streams: a vision for *total restoration* in the Church and a vision for *world evangelisation* by the Church. The prerequisites for Christ's coming fall under either of these streams and God will give specific mandates to His people to accomplish specific aspects of these requirements.

Total Restoration: Our Lord Jesus Christ *"must remain in heaven until the time comes for God to restore everything (all things - KJV)"* (Acts 3:21). There is, therefore, a need for vision in the following areas:

1. Restoration of "The Faith": This is the comprehension and declaration of the total counsel of God as revealed by and through God's holy "apostles and prophets" (Romans 16:25,26; Ephesians 2:19,20; 3:4,5; 2 Peter 3:2), as opposed to meagre portions of it that a lot of believers understand today. Paul was committed to presenting "the word of God in its fullness" to the saints (Colossians 1:25; see also Acts 20:27), in particular the mystery of the unity of both Jews and Gentiles *in* Christ. The "five-fold ministry" has a mandate to equip believers in the truth, that is, in the understanding of "the faith" (Ephesians 4:11,13); we have been given a strong admonition "to contend for *the faith* that was once for all entrusted to" us (Jude 3). Apostles, prophets and teachers are needed today, people who will abandon popular theology and run with a vision to impact the Church with a knowledge of "the faith." (A full exposition on the revelation of the mysteries of the faith is beyond the scope of this book).

2. Restoration of Kingdom life: On a personal and corporate level, it has always been necessary for God to revive that which lies inactive in the Body of Christ. A "dying" Church cannot affect a "dead" world. Revival, in this context, encompasses a return to God and His word, unrestrained allegiance to the revelation of God's principles, and a manifestation of God's love and power in every dimension of life. God will raise ministries with a vision to equip and release believers to walk victoriously in this life.

3. Restoration of Relationships: Before Christ comes, it is evident, as mentioned earlier, that God wants "the hearts of the fathers to [turn] to their children, and the hearts of the children to [turn] to their fathers" (Malachi 4:5,6). In other words, God wants broken relationships mended. Again, this is applicable on personal and corporate levels. In this modern society, parents, fathers in particular, need to be restored to their children; the young and the old need to turn their hearts to one another; even nations need to turn to each other in a spirit of forgiveness and reconciliation. All these are part of the total restoration mandate, and vision is needed to accomplish them.

4. Restoration of the Earth: "The [whole] creation," the Bible says, "waits in eager expectation for the sons of God to be revealed. For the creation was subjected to frustration, not by its own choice, but by the will of the one who subjected it, in hope that the creation itself will be liberated from its bondage to decay and brought into the glorious freedom of the children of God" (Romans 8:19-21). The Spirit of God will inspire, before Christ comes, specific prophetic activity that will lead to the liberation of earthly life. The culmination of this will fully manifest during the coming millennium reign of Christ, when "the wolf and the lamb will feed together, and the lion will eat straw like the ox" (Isaiah 66:25).

World Evangelisation: Of the two streams of *kairos* conditions, world evangelisation is probably the better understood by believers (not necessarily the better obeyed!). God will continue to give His people a vision for missions to the ends of the earth. Until all the ethnic groupings and sub-cultures of the world have an opportunity to hear and respond to the gospel, Christ cannot come. More labourers are therefore needed to run with a Macedonian call to the nations. We have the benefit of research that shows the exact number of un-reached people groups, where they are and how best they can be reached. A vision for completion will especially focus on these remaining fields.

The integration of all God-given visions ultimately fulfils the Great Commission.

Although, the preaching of the gospel in all nations of the earth is the responsibility of the entire Church today, God, the Master Strategist, does give His people specific visions that contribute significantly to its fulfilment. These visions will differ on the basis of geography, strategy, and other determining factors.

We can easily see the need for this because the world has grown in every respect since the first century after Christ. There are now more people, more cultures and sub-cultures, more technologies, more behavioural patterns, more sin etc. The list is unending. The good news is that the resources to reach this multi-faceted world have also increased. The Holy Spirit is stirring up more creative ideas in His people, ideas that have the potential of bringing in the harvest.

If the Great Commission is the Mandate upon the whole Church, then individual visions from God are sections of the Mandate. The integration of all God-given visions ultimately fulfils the Great Commission. No single vision can accomplish the Great Commission. No single person can minister to the whole world. As an individual or a local church, you are called to reach and minister to a specific "people" and accomplish specific results.

We all have specific contributions to the programme of God. If we diligently do the work God assigns to each of us, the overall mandate will speed up astoundingly. No part of the Great Commission should go unattended.

DEGREES OF INVOLVEMENT

Two thoughts are appropriate here. *First,* God will not excuse anyone who chooses indifference to the work of the Kingdom in these last days. We cannot claim *not* to be called. If we search well, we will find our place in God.

The specificity of vision and the complexity of our world imply that there is a mandate God wants to envision *you* for, one that fulfils sections of the two *kairos* conditions. When God gave gifts to men He had you in mind. There is an area of service He has reserved just for you.

> "But all these worketh that one and the selfsame Spirit, *dividing to every man* severally as he will" (1 Corinthians 12:11 KJV *emphasis added*).

> "We have different gifts, according to the grace given us" (Romans 12:6).

> "Each one should use whatever gift he has received to serve others, faithfully administering God's grace in its *various forms*" (1 Peter 4:10 *emphasis added*).

God has a vision for your life that He wants you to run with. Do you know it yet? Are you running with it? No vision from God is insignificant. We tend to give the greater ovation to visible tasks, whereas God honours all and will reward all equally - whatever He has called us to do (see Matthew 20:1-16; 1 Samuel 30:21-25).

In his book, *Serving as Senders*, Neal Pirolo noted that for every front-line missionary serving in the mission field, at least nine other people are needed to give support "at home". The support required includes moral, logistics, financial, prayer, communication and re-entry support. Certainly, there is a place for the "goer" and the "sender"; there is a place for *you*.

The specificity of vision and the complexity of our world imply that there is a mandate God wants to envision *you* for.

The *second* thought is that Scriptures give some indication that God's call upon our lives will not be exclusive to one stream, but rather inclusive of both - in varying degrees. The degree can also change per time according to His will. Our major function may be in the *total restoration* stream but we will be required to contribute to the *world evangelisation* stream in one way or the other (and vice versa).

Paul exhorted Timothy: "do the work of an evangelist [and] discharge all the duties of *your* ministry" (2 Timothy 4:5 *emphasis added*). In other words, even though Timothy was not called to be an "Evangelist", he was expected to do the work of an Evangelist alongside the work of *his* ministry of pastoring and teaching (the *total restoration* stream if you like). We would all have a measure of both streams flowing in us, with one, very likely, being the dominant sense of call.

How many times have you listened to an Evangelist or Missionary and at the end conclude (with traces of guilt) that evangelism is all that God thinks about! A week after, you hear a prophet speak and you are convinced that God only cares about the state of His Church! These tensions are eliminated when we see the bigger picture - God is concerned about the Church *and* is equally concerned about those who are yet to join the Church. We will all embody varying degrees of these concerns depending on the call He has placed on our lives.

The *Holiday Outreach 1991* programme we held in Nigeria had two clear objectives, akin to the two streams discussed above. It combined *outreach* to the town where the programme was held, and *in-reach* to the believers who participated. God had in mind the salvation of sinners and the envisioning of saints. Sinners did get saved and the believers were also challenged. One lady, Lola Amori (nee Omole) received her call to missions during the programme. She is now, together with her husband, serving as missionaries to the Republic of Niger.

I discovered a partnership between the two streams and how they should interrelate. My point of entry to this mission was from the "prophetic" while the point of entry of my friend, Chimezie, with whom the programme was coordinated, was from the "evangelistic". And instead of these two

"giftings" competing or combating, they comple-
mented each other beautifully. Later, Chimezie
would say to me, "It is better you concentrate on
being a 'voice' in the Church if that is what the
Lord has called you to be". After many years, this
counsel still makes sense to me (in the context of
interrelating with evangelistic streams).

PERSONAL AND ORGANISATIONAL VISION

Let us recall God's pattern for advancing His
purpose: He lays hold of a man and the man lays
hold of the Kingdom. When God lays hold on a
person, He impresses visions upon the person's
heart and entrusts him with the responsibility of
running with it. This responsibility involves the
mobilisation of others whom the Lord has ordained
to *run* together in pursuit of the vision. In other
words, individuals discover the vision God has
placed upon them and then they develop it for the
participation of others in the Church. In this way,
everyone is busy - both the visionary and the
people who themselves discover *their* personal
vision *in* the person's vision.

For every cutting-edge establishment, be it a
"church" or "para-church" organisation, there is a
visionary founder who is the person (and sometimes, the people) God used to start the organisation. Hundreds of impacting establishments exist
today with specific visions that contribute significantly to the well-being of humanity and, ultimately,
God's agenda. Any attempt to list names will not

suffice. Heaven, assuredly, has the records and reserves the rewards.

There is no movement or organisation that did not start as an idea in someone's mind; better still, as a word from the Lord in the heart. The ages have truly been framed by specific words from God (Hebrews 11:3). We need more people who will humbly receive fresh vision from God and develop it for the participation of others.

If every pastor develops a God-given vision for his local assembly, we will see church members running with great momentum to the ends of the earth, fulfilling the mandate upon the assembly and upon their lives. This is part of what Jesus Christ had in mind when he "gave gifts unto men" for the purpose of preparing "God's people for works of service" (Ephesians 4:7-13). Which means that apart from teaching and instructing the believers, leaders have the task of equipping them with the ability to discover *their* vision in the vision, and encouraging them to glorify God by running with it. The absence of this will produce lethargic church members and a lukewarm congregation.

In these last days, God wants every believer running with a vision and not standing in confusion!

Vision directs; it points to *where* we should run.

The Spirit imparts; He gives the strength with *which* we can to run.

Jesus Christ motivates; He is the reason *why* we run.

The Father rewards; He guarantees that our running will not be in vain.

If every pastor develops a God-given vision for his local assembly, we will see church members running with great momentum to the ends of the earth, fulfilling the mandate upon the assembly and upon their lives.

A word of caution is relevant here. Jesus Christ is the sole Head and Visionary of the Church. He said clearly, "*I* will build *my* Church" (Matthew 16:18 *emphasis added*). We all, no matter the nature of our calling, are part of *His* building. He alone is the Chief Cornerstone and we are "lively stones... being built into a spiritual house to be a holy priesthood, offering spiritual sacrifices acceptable to God through Jesus Christ" (1 Peter 2:5). The Church, the body *of* Christ, belongs to no man but to Christ. The ministry of the Church, also, is not the ministry of anyone, but the ministry of Christ. It is through "the Church", in its local and global expressions, that Christ accomplishes *His* ministry to the world. We all have the privilege of having *a ministry* within *His Ministry*.

The reason why this caution is crucial is that in recent times, local church ministries (and para-church ministries), generally speaking, have been regarded as belonging to the mortal visionaries whom the Lord used to start them. We seem to claim ownership of the work that belongs to God. In our minds we "own" the work. We also "own" all the resources available for the work - the people, the money and everything else. The vision of the church plant has become the sole vision of its founder and everyone works to promote it at all costs (actually, promote him or her as the case may be).

This entrepreneur mindset is a major bottleneck hindering our swift movement towards finishing God's work. It gives birth to territorialism, competitiveness, self-promotion and a catalogue of other anti-kingdom practices. It stifles the multiplication of *Christ's ministry* in the earth, hinders the flow of resources (be it finance, ideas, ministries etc) from one part of the body to another, and slows down the Church's growth, fruitfulness and productivity. (By saying "Christ's ministry", I refer to the functioning of God's people and not the registering of NGOs!).

Every true vision that is worth its weight in eternity is not about the visionary but about Christ. As the chorus goes:

> It's all about you
> Nothing else matters

That a person is leading a Christian establishment does not make him or her the Alpha and Omega of a little empire. Leaders have been called and gifted as everyone else. They have a responsibility (and in many ways, a greater responsibility) to be faithful in their calling as everyone else.

> "We have different gifts, according to the grace given us. If a man's gift is prophesying, let him use it in proportion to his faith. If it is serving, let him serve; if it is teaching, let him teach; if it is encouraging, let him encourage; if it is contributing to the needs of others, let him give generously; *if it is leadership, let him govern diligently*; if it is showing mercy, let him do it cheerfully" (Romans 12:6-8 *emphasis added*).

> "Not many of you should presume to be teachers, my brothers, because you know that *we who teach will be judged more strictly*" (James 3:1 *emphasis added*).

If we maintain the dual focus of the Christian life discussed earlier, with love for God *and* His people being a priority over our individual callings, some of these bottlenecks will easily be isolated and the purposes of God will advance towards completion.

MORE INSIGHT ON VISION

Let us summarise all of these insights on vision (and probably add a bit more!) by considering a familiar portion of Scripture.

"I [Habakkuk] will stand upon my watch, and set me upon the tower, and will watch to see what he will say unto me, and what I shall answer when I am reproved. And the LORD answered me, and said, Write the vision, and make it plain upon tablets, that he may run that readeth it. For the vision is yet for an appointed time, but at the end it shall speak, and shall not lie: though it tarry, wait for it because it will surely come, it will not tarry" (Habakkuk 2:1-3 KJV).

1. Vision must be received from God.

God-given visions are *God-given*. Many so-called visions today were received from men or from books. No wonder why they can hardly produce momentum in others. If the Lord does not speak, no-one can speak for Him. Moreover, "no-one takes this honour upon himself; he must be called by God, just as Aaron was" (Hebrews 5:4).

In the light of eternal purpose, one specific word from God's heart is better than a hundred and one good ideas from man's mind.

The prophet Habakkuk decided to wait on God until the Lord communicated His mind and divine plan to him. He did not just assume what the mind of God was.

The time invested in waiting on God for a specific sense of purpose is never a waste. True visions are not assumptions but convictions, and convictions come after God speaks. Convictions also grow over time. In the light of eternal purpose, one specific word from God's heart is better than a hundred and one good ideas from man's mind. We all need a visitation from God; a revelation of vision. These will come as we wait on Him.

2. Vision will be discerned in the context of your relationship with God.

In the interim, while waiting on God, get busy with Kingdom work - whatever your hand finds to do! Continue to walk with God in holiness and uprightness. God will not give end-time visions to idle souls. He will not share His heart with believers that are not committed to living in the truth of His word (see 2 Timothy 3:16,17). As we shared earlier in this chapter, you will discover God's vision for your life as you develop your relationship with Him and with the Body of Christ. The success of vision is dependent on the strength of your character, and a strong character is a result of a strong relationship with God, His word and His people.

Habakkuk, it seems, was not waiting on God just for a vision. He presented himself to God wanting to see if God had anything to reprove in his life (verse 1). In the process of his "soul-searching", the vision came. Similarly, king David was just expressing his desire to honour God when He discovered God's plan for his life and for his descendants (see 2 Samuel 7). Great visions come to those who selflessly give themselves to God's service without any desire to be lord over others.

3. Vision will be discerned in the context of your gift and talent mix.

In the process of walking with God open-heartedly, getting involved in His service, God will give you a deeper insight into what He has invested in you - gifts, talents and abilities. True vision will not contradict your personality make-up. These two will normally be compatible with each other. Your natural and spiritual gifts are important in the pursuit of vision.

Great visions come to those who selflessly give themselves to God's service without any desire to be lord over others.

Heavenly visions are unique because God has uniquely gifted everyone. No two people are the same. A God-given vision will define your purpose in life and demand total attention. The ultimate in vision pursuit is when you and your vision for life become inseparable. That is, when the vision becomes the reason why God made you the way you are.

4. Vision will be communicated as a response to direct enquiry.

After Habakkuk decided to wait on God, the Bible says that "the LORD answered [him] and said...". This presumes that Habakkuk asked God some fitting questions (see Habakkuk 1). A great secret in discovering vision is to ask God questions.

Many believers today do not know the power of "direct enquiry" in prayer. Asking questions from the right person is not a sign of dumbness, but a great display of wisdom. God will usually respond to direct enquiry, more so if it has to do with the advancement of His purpose. He said, "Call unto me, and I will *answer* thee, and shew thee great and mighty things, which thou knowest not" (Jeremiah 33:3 KJV *emphasis added*).

The fulfilment of God's divine purposes integrates the callings He has placed upon every individual in His Kingdom. Therefore, the desire you have to know God's will for your life has direct consequences on the fulfilment of God's purpose at large.

Moses came into a revelation of his destiny because of his inquisitiveness.

> "So Moses thought, 'I will go over and
> see this strange sight - why the bush

does not burn up'. *When the LORD saw that he had gone over to look,* God called to him from within the bush, 'Moses! Moses!'. And Moses said, 'Here I am'" (Exodus 3:3,4 *emphasis added*).

Saul, the son of Kish, was on his way to ask prophet Samuel some questions when he "bumped" into his destiny as the first king of Israel. King David knew the power of questioning God. He almost never did anything without asking for God's opinion.

Who have I been designed to reach and bless? How can I contribute to the accomplishment of Your purposes in my generation?

God brought me into some incredible revelations about my destiny when I cried out to Him: *What shall this man do?* The mandate to organise the *Holiday Outreach* programme I have shared about earlier in this book came as God's immediate response to this enquiry.

Ask God leading questions about your purpose in life. Find out the answers to questions like: *Why am I here? What do I desire most in life? What do I love most? What do I not love doing at all?* (God will hardly ask us to do something that we cannot develop a desire and a love for). *What excites me?*

What puts me off? What am I good at? What am I not good at? What angers me and stirs my passion? What fills my conversation and thoughts? What thing can I spend the rest of my life doing without feeling bored? If I had unlimited resources, what project will I embark upon? God, why have you created me? Who have I been designed to reach and bless? How can I contribute to the accomplishment of Your purposes in my generation? How can I best bring glory to your name? O God, What shall this man do!

Answers to questions like these can give vital hints on your purpose in life. Sooner or later, the Lord will enlighten your heart as to what He has called you to be and do.

5. *Vision must be written.*

God told Habakkuk to "write the vision". The truth is, you do not have a vision until it is written. Do you understand what God wants to use you for well enough to jot it down in a few sentences? Is the vision of your local Church only verbalised and not inscribed?

The benefits of writing are tremendous. Even God has different books for different purposes. He diligently writes down the things that matter to Him in their appropriate books. Even though God cannot forget things, He still writes them down. The written word is proof that the written thought exists. Since we *do* forget things, it is wise for God, then, to instruct us to write the vision He gives.

Inspiration comes to the "hearing heart" but stays with the "ready writer". Many people lose divine ideas because of a lackadaisical attitude to writing. A short pen, it is said, is better than a long memory. Jot down the thoughts that come to you from God and filter them through the word of God and transparent motives. They may represent key ideas that will unlock your destiny and bring about a speedy fulfilment of God's will for your life.

6. Vision must be plain.

Not only should you write down your God-given vision, you must also make it plain. In other words, develop the vision you discover in God. Does your Church have "what", "why" and "how" statements that explain what the ministry stands for and what it is commissioned to achieve? It is not enough to glean insight about vision. Further details are essential if others will participate in its fulfilment. *What* do you want to do? *How* do you want to do it? *Where* do you want to do it? *When* do you want to do it? *With whom* do you want to do it? *For how long* do you want to do it? These details fine-tune vision and sharpen focus. They leave no-one in doubt as to what is being aimed for.

Vision development requires the investment of time, but it also pays great dividends.

You are not ready, of course, to make a vision plain if it has not become a part of you. When God's directive is *plain* upon the tablets of your heart and comprehended fully in your mind it will "easily" transcribe unto paper.

Vision development requires the investment of time, but it also pays great dividends. With an understanding that your vision is your unique contribution to the extension of the God's Kingdom, stir up yourself and invest the necessary time to establish its details.

7. *Vision must be communicated.*

The make-it-plain phase of vision development is not just for the sake of the writer, but for benefit of the reader. A well-developed vision from God will inspire those that peruse it and generate in them a desire to run in the direction that the vision points.

Vision must be communicated to others. It generates momentum in the Church. It mobilises believers and provokes their involvement. It enlists prayer partners and financial supporters (people will give to vision and visionaries, not just to need). It causes believers to run in the same direction and for the same purpose.

More than ever, we need the whole Church running towards the completion of God's purpose. For this to happen, we need well-articulated visions in every section of the Lord's camp.

8. *Vision must be pursued... with patience.*

Vision generates momentum. However, God was careful to add the dimension of patience to the impetus: "though it tarry, *wait for it* because it will surely come, it will not tarry". The writer of Hebrews expresses this same thought.

> "Let us *run with perseverance* the race marked out for us" (Hebrews 12:1b *emphasis added*).

A well-developed vision from God will inspire those that peruse it and generate in them a desire to run in the direction that the vision points.

When God gives a vision, it comes with a strong this-can-be-done-now sensation! However, God will have us to wait for Him and not run off in our own strength. Even though time is short and God is doing a quick work, we still need to wait on Him and be led by Him. God uses this *spiritual tension* to keep us dependent on Him. He also uses it to guarantee ultimate success. Vision will require that we give our very lives in its pursuit, but God has given His word that vision that comes from Him will not fail.

God is the Creator of time but He is not bound by it. In the time-frame we find ourselves, no matter how short it seems, we can wait for God and simultaneously be persuaded that God's word will come to pass.

> "There is a time for everything, and a season for every activity under heaven... [God] has made everything beautiful in its time" (Ecclesiastes 3:1,11a).

The time-dimension of vision has been violated by many. This, in some cases, is the cause of ineffectiveness and failure in vision execution. Saul, the first king of Israel, jeopardised his leadership position by missing the timing God set for him (1 Samuel 13:8-14). At the fullness of time, after training and preparation, God will use His faithful vessels to bring an end to the end-time mandate. "Though it linger, wait for it; it will certainly come and it will not delay".

Even though time is short and God is doing a quick work, we still need to wait on Him and be led by Him.

*****

Young men shall indeed see visions! Fresh, innovative and creative contributions to the divine mandate! We cannot do without them in these crucial days.

Vision is the best antidote for tradition. It is an end-time necessity. No assembly should satisfy itself with ministry without direction. Activity will be aimless if vision in absent. Passion will gradually wane without the inspiration of vision.

Remember, also, that the target of vision must not only be specific, but also relevant. Any stated vision that does not contribute to God's purpose is not a part of the integrated whole. The significance and relevance of vision is its contribution to God's mission. It is *His* mission that gives birth to *our* vision. No vision should exist outside God's divine purpose. This is the foundation of unity. If we *truly* have one purpose, our visions will *complement* and *contribute to* one another. Purpose arrests the spirit of *competition* and subjects it to the will of Christ.

Everything we do must reflect the purpose of God for these last days. The world has to be reached and the Church prepared for the coming of Jesus Christ. This is our destiny as a people of God. Its completion will bring glory to our Saviour Jesus Christ. May we arise at this time and run with all the strength available in God - as *fast* as we can run and as *far* as we see.

> "To this end I labour, struggling with all his energy, which so powerfully works in me" (Colossians 1:29).

> "Tell Archippus: 'See to it that you *complete the work* (vision) you have received in the Lord" (Colossians 4:19 *emphasis added*).

PART 3

THE URGENCY
OF THE HOUR

8 | THE MYSTERY OF DIVINE ACCELERATION

What time are we living in? How far are we from the close of the age of grace? How much time do we have left for the accomplishment of God's purposes?

We have heard of the last days, but are actually in the *last* of the last days. We have heard of the end-times, but are in the *end* of the end-times. There is no more time to play around. We cannot afford to ignore the purposes of God and our unfinished mandate anymore.

Those who are sensitive in the realms of the spirit will realise that Bible prophecies are coming to pass at a very staggering rate. The physical world is also changing rapidly. Many have lost touch with what is really happening in the world. This is how fast things are changing.

THE WORLD IS PREPARING FOR THE ANTICHRIST

A lot of the shifts occurring in the world today are in preparation for the "Man of Lawlessness", the Antichrist who will rule the coming One World Government. The appearance of this world ruler is actually one of the *kairos* conditions for the coming of Christ!

> *"Concerning the coming of our Lord Jesus Christ and our being gathered to him,* we ask you, brothers, not to become easily unsettled or alarmed by some prophecy, report or letter supposed to have come from us, saying that the day of the Lord has already come. Don't let anyone deceive you in any way, *for that day will not come **until** the rebellion occurs and the man of lawlessness is revealed, the man doomed to destruction"* (2 Thessalonians 2:1-3 *emphasis added*).

There is an ongoing process of global restructuring. Economically, politically and religiously, the stage is being set for the rise of the Antichrist. Prophecy is unfolding before our very eyes every single day. A cashless society is now feasible. Technology for the electronic mark of the beast is already in use. The Internet has turned the world into a global village. The microchip industry is still developing rapidly. These technological break-throughs, not to mention those in biochemical, medical and other fields, continue to fulfil God's word to Daniel: *Knowledge shall increase.*

The threat of global terrorism has increased the quest for security and peace around the world. Instead of peace, there are more wars and multi-plied fear. September 11 has changed the face of the world forever. Weapons of mass destruction can, indeed, be a common feature if global breaks out, leading to the annihilation of entire cities at a time.

These are not end-time fairy tales neither are they apocalyptic jargon. Books about "the end of days" are one the fast selling titles today. The Church needs to wake up to the realities of her generation. We are living in the end of time and "time", as we know it, is ticking away everyday! These are the days of prophetic fulfilment. God's eternal purpose is winding to a speedy end.

Those who are sensitive in the realms of the spirit will realise that Bible prophecies are coming to pass at a very staggering rate.

Now, if all these predictions are not failing, how can we expect the coming of Christ or the end of the world not to come to pass as foretold? Jesus

Christ is coming again. He will soon stand up from His throne and gather the saints to Himself. The mouth of the Lord has spoken it; His zeal will accomplish it.

ROUNDING UP TIMES

Once again, what time are we living in?

The end-times?

Yes, but more than the end-times.

The last days?

Yes, but more than the last days.

The time of the latter rain?

Yes, but more than the time of the latter rain.

Are we living in the time of revival, refreshing, reformation, restoration, reconciliation or restitution?

Yes, all of these, but our season is much more significant and specific.

While these "re"-words describe our era, we still need a greater degree of accuracy in order to focus on *finishing* the works of God. Our attention needs to be more rapt than it has ever been. In the context of the message in this book, the following sentence, probably, sums up the era in which we live:

> We are living in *Rounding Up Times*, the days when God will fully accomplish everything He purposed for our age.

Remember that purpose always defines a beginning and an end (see chapter 1). The world in which we live had a beginning and it will have an end. This means that without any further delay, every proclamation that God had made concerning the earth should be executed in its time.

> "Then the angel I had seen standing on the sea and on the land raised his right hand to heaven. And he swore by him who lives for ever and ever, who created the heavens and all that is in them, the earth and all that is in it, and the sea and all that is in it, and said, *'There will be no more delay!* But in the days when the seventh angel is about to sound his trumpet, *the mystery of God will be accomplished*, just as he announced to his servants the prophets'" (Revelation 10:6,7 *emphasis added*).

God's longsuffering is meant to bring men and women into the Kingdom, but after the "fullness of the gentiles" come in, His patience would fully accomplish its purpose. At the fullness of time God will send Jesus to round up the final part of His purpose - the eternal judgement of sin, Satan and death.

THE SPEEDING UP OF TIME

The Bible says, "the Lord will carry out his sentence on the earth with speed and finality" (Romans 9:28). This means that God is not just out to round up His plans, He is also doing it with "speed and finality". This is why things seem to be moving fast all around us. There is a sense of urgency that the spiritually sensitive cannot deny.

This means that without any further delay, every proclamation that God had made concerning the earth should be executed in its time.

Church, it is time to run! It is time to accelerate! In a little while, "time" will cease to exist. We need to spend the little time that we have left wisely for the advancement of the Kingdom of God.

> "Be very careful, then, how you live - not as unwise but as wise, *making the most of every opportunity*, because the days are evil. Therefore do not be foolish, but understand what the Lord's will is" (Ephesians 5:15-17 *emphasis added*).

The will of God is the fulfilment of His purpose. It is therefore unwise to live without a sense of purpose, destiny and urgency.

CHURCH WAKE UP!

As we have established earlier, the Church has a major role to play in rounding up of the purposes of God in the earth. We are the ones through whom the Holy Spirit will establish a witness in every nation before the coming of the Lord. Just as John the Baptist was responsible for preparing the way for Christ's first advent, we, the Body of Christ, are also responsible for preparing the way for His second coming.

> "A voice of one calling: 'In the desert prepare the way for the LORD; make straight in the wilderness a highway for our God. Every valley shall be raised up, every mountain and hill made low; the rough ground shall become level, the rugged places a plain. And the glory of the LORD will be revealed and all mankind together will see it. For the mouth of the LORD has spoken'" (Isaiah 40:3-5).

God needs a "highway" for the move of His Spirit and not a crooked, narrow path of religious tradition. If the glory of the Lord will break forth upon the earth, then the Church, the supposed carrier of this glory, must arise and shine for God (Isaiah 60:1,2). All the things that obstruct the Lord's path, especially amongst Church leaders, must be eradicated. Gossip, negative criticism, disunity, envy, unnecessary strife, and all the ugly works of the flesh will not allow for a move of the

Spirit in the Church. They would constitute stumbling blocks on the revival highway. It is high time we woke up from sleep so that the world may see the glory of our God.

> "Wake up, O sleeper, rise from the dead, and Christ will shine on you" (Ephesians 5:14).

A FRESH ANOINTING

These are the days of God's power, the time of the final revival. God is releasing a fresh anointing upon His sons and daughters. It is an anointing for the rounding up of prophecy; an anointing to restore the broken walls and re-establish the faith; an anointing to run to the battle and conquer the enemy. God's anointing always has a purpose for manifesting. This fresh outpouring will bring every iota of God's word to pass before our very eyes.

God needs a "highway" for the move of His Spirit and not a crooked, narrow path of religious tradition.

By the anointing, the Church will walk in revelation (Ephesians 1:17). Through revelation and wisdom, the Church will walk in dominion wherever she turns. The enemies of God will be subdued and Christ will come gloriously for His glorious people.

Together with the anointing will come a fresh impartation of strength. We will *run* with amazing speed, fulfilling the purposes of God. Wisdom and revelation will be our rear guard; grace and favour our front guard; and the glory of God will be our light. Multitudes will flock into the Kingdom of God; the nations will come into the brightness of our light (Isaiah 60). Every principle in the Word of God will become a functional reality in the Church. The long-awaited sons of God will manifest for the world to see (Romans 8:19). All this shall happen because of a divine mystery that will be at work in our time: *The Mystery of Divine Acceleration*. This mystery will accompany the fresh anointing of God's Spirit.

> "The least of you will become a thousand, the smallest a mighty nation. I am the LORD; *in its time I will do this swiftly*" (Isaiah 60:22 *emphasis added*).

KEEPING IN STEP WITH GOD

God is not waiting for us to get ready at this time. He has already waited for more than 2,000 years! He expects our generation (with our over-abundant accumulation of resources) to key into this anointing and finish His work. The spiritually sensitive and those who are ready will move ahead with God. Many others will have to play "catch up"; they will struggle to keep in step with the move of God.

The world is moving fast, but God will overtake the world. If, truly, the governments of the world are preparing for the antichrist, then, we too, through the *Mystery of Divine Acceleration*, must aggressively prepare for our coming Christ. We must keep in step with what God is doing in our world and co-operate with Him by obeying every instruction that He gives.

God is directly responsible for the speeding up of time. Our task is to flow with the mainstream of God's divine activity. When we make ourselves available for God's use, He will bring great things to pass through our lives. Through divine revelation and a strong focus on purpose, we can move ahead in the things of God with divine swiftness.

If, truly, the governments of the world are preparing for the antichrist, then, we too must aggressively prepare for our coming Christ.

THE LIGHT OF REVELATION

The finish-line of history and destiny is in clear view. Now is the time to quicken the coming of Christ. There is a *kind* of lifestyle we can live that will affect the timing of this event. Apostle Peter gave this hint in his second epistle to the Church.

> "Since everything will be destroyed in this way, what kind of people ought you to be? *You ought to live holy and godly lives as you look forward to the day of God and speed its coming*" (2 Peter 3:11,12 *emphasis added*).

The lifestyle referred to here is the *Bible* lifestyle. Living in the light of Biblical revelation equips us for every good work God has ordained for us (see 2 Timothy 3:16,17; Philippians 1:9-11; Colossians 1:9-12). Purity, unity, the fear of God and every written counsel of God should not be a struggle for anyone serious about the coming of Christ.

As the Lord opens the eyes of the Church to treasures in the Scriptures, and the Church commits herself to willingness and total obedience, great things will happen across the nations. The *farther* we see in the spirit, the *faster* we can move towards the finish line. The clearer our spiritual perception, the more accurate our decisions. We cannot operate beyond our understanding of God's word. We cannot go beyond the light that we have. Paul did so much in so little a time because He was a man of revelation. O that the Lord will pour out His Spirit of revelation upon us afresh!

> "Your word is a lamp to my feet and a lamp to my feet... The entrance and unfolding of Your words give light; their

unfolding gives understanding (discernment and comprehension) to the simple" (Psalm 119:105,130 Amp *additions mine*).

Convictions about the final seasons of human existence were firmly impressed upon me by revelation barely two days after my conversion. Although I was a teenager with a limited understanding of spiritual things, it pleased God to bless me with insight and a gift to write. For nineteen hours, I wrote things about the last days that were being unveiled in my heart. The revelations that were flooding through my spirit seemed like the unfolding of an endless scroll.

Some have heard me recount this experience or have read it from the author's profile behind some of my books, but I seldom share about the contents of what I wrote. The truth is, a week after the experience, the writings were deposited with the late Dr. I.K.U. Ibeneme, founder of *Faith Clinic* in Nigeria. No-one could understand what was happening to me, hence leaving the book with him felt safe.

In retrospect, I am grateful for not being in possession of the original notebook because my faith needed to be based on God's word and not just an unusual experience. Nonetheless, at least two lines of thought that emerged from those writings have stayed with me ever since.

The first revelation was that the church does not need more than a single, willing generation to round up the prophecies and purposes of God. If "the end" will come *after* the gospel of the kingdom reaches the ends of the earth, how many "Pauls" or "Peters" are necessary to finish the work? What about the acceleration that will occur when the church is completely united? What about the luxury of using resources that were not available centuries ago? These were the questions that came to me the day after my conversion. I actually took a calculator and computed the rate of increase of the church in the book of Acts - from 120 to 3,000, to 5,000, until the entire "world" of that time was turned upside down in one generation! The Lord's argument was that only a few people (potentially the whole church!) with the *passion* and *motivation* of Paul is enough for the job *in one generation*. Sadly, true Pauls are scarce.

The second insight that stayed with me since the writing encounter was the role of deliverance in proclaiming the gospel of the kingdom and the necessity of this ministry for cleansing in the church. While I am aware of the different reactions people have to the practice of casting out devils, these were the messages that were downloaded into my spirit and relayed through writing.

Although I was young in age, the light of revelation accelerated my growth in the spirit. Barely a year into my new life in Christ, I began to share God's word and cast out devils! Such are the effects of what I call *The Mystery of Divine Acceleration!* Unprecedented transformations will occur in our lives and ministries as we receive light from heaven and align ourselves with God's word.

INSIGHTS FOR DIVINE ACCELERATION

It is my conviction that divine revelation is a key to spiritual acceleration. It is also the birthplace of vision. Paul was a man with a mission because He was a man of revelation (see Galatians 1:11-12; 2:1-2). You may not have an experience like the one I had, but you are still a candidate for divine light from the word of God. The Holy Scriptures is the primary place from which God's light beams.

In my book *Rediscovering God,* I wrote the following:

> "Perhaps I should stress once again that what I refer to here as revelation is not a dream, trance or any such thing. God may surely speak through these (and he does) but the word of God is the surer and primary foundation. The understanding that the Holy Spirit gives from the word - cumulative knowledge of the will and mind of God - resulting in fresh insights into the heart and nature of God, His laws and commandments, is the revelation I am writing about." (pg. 31)

If we would run the course of God's commands, we need God's word to explode in our hearts. Only God's word can move us speedily from where we are to where He wants us to be; it will set our hearts free from stagnation and tradition.

We can all relate to times when we have been impacted by insight that someone shared from

God's word. Such is the power of Scripture! We need to increase the practice of sharing God's word with each other, particularly, in this rounding-up season. It was the word that began this age and it will be the word that will bring it to an end. There is fresh insight available for "download" from heaven! Anyone holding unto the manna of yesterday may become unusable in executing the holy purposes of God.

It is my conviction that divine revelation is a key to spiritual acceleration. It is also the birthplace of vision.

In this section, I will share some insight from the word of God that, hopefully, will inspire and motivate you in the pursuit of God's purpose. They will produce fire in your bones and urge you to move on in God. They will affect your present mentality and tune you into the Holy Spirit's current frequency of operation. They will line you up with God's agenda for your life. Certainly not an exhaustive list, these insights relate to *The Mystery of Divine Acceleration* that is at work today.

When God's word is alive in you, it will propel you to do God's work. Let these insights act as fuel that will set your heart ablaze for God and renew your mind for end-time activity.

Insight #1: Total Obedience

> "'Dear woman, why do you involve
> me?', Jesus replied, 'My time has not yet
> come'. His mother said to the servants,
> 'Do whatever he tells you'" (John 2:4,5).

Jesus said it was not yet time for miracles, but
Mary sped up the time by positioning herself to
obey any command He might give.

Miracles - quick, accelerated and unprecedented
miracles - happen when we dare to obey the
commands of Christ to the letter. Some commands
may seem illogical, but obedience will release the
miracle. We can speed up the time of Christ's
manifestation by doing whatever His Spirit
instructs us.

**Specific obedience releases
specific grace and accom-
plishes specific exploits.**

Everywhere people obeyed God in the Bible,
purpose advanced. Disobedience slows down
the execution of God's counsel. The essence of
instructions is to link us to supernatural supply. Its
purpose is defeated when it is not followed up with
obedience. If we are willing and obedient in these
last days, we will possess the land for the Lord.

Insight #2: Specific Direction

> "Paul and his companions travelled throughout the region of Phrygia and Galatia, *having been kept by the Holy Spirit from preaching the word in the province of Asia.* When they came to the border of Mysia, they tried to enter Bithynia, but the Spirit of Jesus would not allow them to. So they passed by Mysia and went down to Troas. During the night Paul had a vision of a man of Macedonia standing and begging him, 'Come over to Macedonia and help us'. After Paul had seen the vision, we got ready at once to leave for Macedonia, *concluding that God had called us to preach the gospel to them*" (Acts 16:6-10 *emphasis added*).

Even though Christ had said "Go ye into all the world", Paul discovered the need to "Go ye by *a word* from the Lord".   Before we rush to the nations, we may need to "Stay ye *for* a word from the Lord"!

God is a God of specificity. He has a specific instruction for a specific situation, at a specific point in time. Specific obedience releases specific grace and accomplishes specific exploits. A general idea of God's will is commendable, but one must be sensitive to specific direction and instruction from Him. The instructions for crossing River Jordan are different from those for the Red Sea. On

the surface they may seem the same, but results are
only guaranteed when God's specific directions are
followed in each instance.

Do not embark on things because they are popular or convenient. Obey God. Follow His leading.
God does not only give vision; He also gives direction. Sensitivity to God will produce maximum
results in the shortest time possible.

Insight #3: Divine Infusion

> "So he got up and ate and drank.
> *Strengthened by that food*, he travelled for
> forty days and forty nights until he
> reached Horeb, the mountain of
> God" (1 Kings 19:8 *emphasis added*).

> "But my horn shalt thou exalt like the
> horn of an unicorn: *I shall be anointed
> with fresh oil*" (Psalm 92:10 KJV *emphasis
> added*).

> "But they that wait upon the LORD
> shall renew their strength; *they shall
> mount up* with wings as eagles; *they shall
> run*, and not be weary; and *they shall
> walk*, and not faint" (Isaiah 40:31 KJV
> *emphasis added*).

We cannot depend upon the strength of yesterday to run the race of today. We need fresh grace
for every lap of our race. Especially in these last
days, those who depend totally on God, waiting on

Him for direction, will experience the strength and agility of an eagle. The methodologies of man cannot last for too long. Only the arm of the Lord will secure lasting victory.

In a fast-paced world, it is sometimes difficult to find time to relax and recuperate strength. In the Church as well, a lot of ministry operations are geared towards the fast lane. Before we all run out of oil, we need to wait on God for fresh unction. If you have to take a break from work, do so before your work breaks you!

Insight #4: Fuel of intercession

"Elijah was a man just like us. *He prayed* earnestly that it would not rain, and it did not rain on the land for three and a half years. *Again he prayed*, and the heavens gave rain, and the earth produced its crops" (James 5:17 *emphasis added*).

"*Ask of me*, and I will make the nations your inheritance, the ends of the earth your possession" (Psalm 2:8 *emphasis added*).

"Then he said to his disciples, 'The harvest is plentiful but the workers are few. *Ask the Lord of the harvest*, therefore, to send out workers into his harvest field'" (Matthew 9:37,38 *emphasis added*).

Intercession advances the purposes of God. Whenever men pray on earth, God moves in heaven. When God moves in heaven, the effects are seen on earth. Could it be that we are not seeing the visible move of God on earth because God cannot hear the audible prayers of men in heaven? The end-time revival will require the fuel of intercession - powerful, purposeful prayers. Targeted prayers produce targeted results. Focused prayers produce focused results. The 40/70 window has become the main mission block of the 21st Century. May we all be motivated to pray down the glory and kingdom of God. May we be inspired to pray directly for total restoration and world evangelisation. The effects will be rapid and visible (Isaiah 62:1,6,7).

Could it be that we are not seeing the visible move of God on earth because God cannot hear the audible prayers of men in heaven?

Insight #5: Focus on Purpose

"I press on to take hold of that for which Christ took hold of me. Brothers, I do not consider myself yet to have taken hold of it. *But one thing I do*: Forgetting what is behind and straining towards what is ahead, I press on towards the goal to win the prize for which God has called me heavenwards in Christ Jesus" (Philippians 3:12-14 *emphasis added*).

For the accomplishment of the divine mandate, God's people must focus on purpose. Vision will fail if focus is broken. The purpose of Satan's temptations in a believer's life is to distract from purpose. We need to label anything that distracts as an enemy of purpose, no matter how legitimate such a distraction may be.

It is wise and better to succeed in one thing than to fail at many. The benefit of a specific vision is specific focus. Focus optimises the use of available resources. When there is a focus on purpose, the most important factor is movement towards it. Every other issue is secondary. The work of the Kingdom will be accomplished in our time if we focus directly on it.

Insight #6: Kingdom Mentality

"Now those who had been scattered by the persecution in connection with Stephen travelled as far as Phoenicia, Cyprus and Antioch, telling the message only to Jews. *Some of them, however, men from Cyprus and Cyrene, went to Antioch and began to speak to Greek also,* telling them the good news about the Lord Jesus. *The Lord's hand*

was with them, and a great number of
people believed and turned to the Lord.
News of this reached the ears of the
Church at Jerusalem, and they sent
Barnabas to Antioch. When he arrived
and saw the evidence of the grace of
God, he was glad and encouraged them
all to remain true to the Lord with all
their hearts... *The disciples were called
Christians first at Antioch"* (Acts 11:19-
23,26b *emphasis added*).

A right focus on purpose affects one's mentality.
In a state of broken focus, other things become
important but the real thing. Kingdom focus will
produce a Kingdom mentality. Disunity is the
highest expression of an anti-kingdom mentality.
Pride and self-promotion follow close behind. The
desire to be known and named is also against kingdom thinking.

The "men from Cyprus and Cyrene" were Kingdom thinkers. They had no desire to be known.
They did not set out to build personal kingdoms,
but were about the building of the Kingdom of
God. Till today, we do not know their names but
their work has outlived them for two millennia.
Heaven will reveal a lot on the day of reckoning.
The popular names of today may not receive the
recognition they presently enjoy. The unknown
may be the first to receive their rewards - and the
best of rewards. The determining factor is motive
and mentality.

We are called "Christians" today because these unsung heroes broke the barriers of tradition to advance the purpose of God. While others were preaching only to fellow Jews, these men crossed cultural barriers and preached Jesus to gentiles. They had the interest of God's Kingdom in their heart and not earthly patriotism.

True Kingdom mentality will break the power of disunity in the Church. These "men from Cyprus and Cyrene" did not consider the input of the Church at Jerusalem, through Barnabas (and later Paul), as a threat or an invasion of their "ministerial territory". They instead welcomed them and their ministry. So far the kingdom of God would benefit they had no objection. Later, Barnabas and Paul were sent forth and supported as missionaries from their midst.

We need this kind of mentality today, no doubt. Nothing is more important than the advance of purpose in our generation, and a restoration of kingdom thinking will get the work done.

Insight #7: Ends-of-the-earth-mentality

> "...So from Jerusalem all the way around to Illycum, I have fully proclaimed the gospel of Christ. It has always been my ambition to preach the gospel *where Christ was not known,* so that I would not be building on someone else's foundation" (Romans 15:19,20 *emphasis added*).

"And when they found him, they exclaimed: 'Everyone is looking for you!' Jesus replied, 'Let us go somewhere else - to the nearby villages - so that I can preach there also. That is why I have come'. *So he travelled throughout Galilee,* preaching in their synagogues and driving out demons" (Mark 1:37-39 *emphasis added*).

"But you will receive power when the Holy Spirit comes on you; and you will be my witnesses in Jerusalem, and in all Judea and Samaria, and *to the ends of the earth*" (Acts 1:8 *emphasis added*).

We have an "ends-of-the-earth" mandate and therefore need an "ends-of-the-earth" mentality. We are called to be pioneers and not settlers; dynamic and not static. The task of reaching the world for Jesus will remain unfinished if we do not have the correct mindset that will spur us, corporately, into every nation on earth.

Insight #8: Kingdom Priority

"But seek ye *first* the kingdom of God, and his righteousness; and all these things shall be added unto you" (Matthew 6:33 KJV *emphasis added*).

It is relatively easier to develop the correct kingdom mentality when kingdom priorities are in place. Instead of making the increase of earthly wealth a priority, Christ taught us to make the advancement of God's Kingdom the most important item on our daily agenda. This is not a one-time attainment but a life-time commitment. "Of the increase of his government and peace *there [should] be no end*", not until all the kingdoms of the earth are brought under the rule of Christ (Isaiah 9:7 *emphasis added*).

Notice that we have to seek two things: "the kingdom of God *and* His righteousness". When we seek the increase of *God's kingdom* (the external domain of Christ's authority), everything will be added to us because of our sense of purpose. When we seek the increase of His *righteousness* (the internal Lordship of Christ in the heart), everything will be added because of our roots in His character. Those who will speedily advance the Kingdom of God will seek first His Kingdom *and* His righteousness.

It is relatively easier to develop the correct kingdom mentality when kingdom priorities are in place.

Insight #9: Financial Abundance

"... The wealth of the sinner is laid up for the just" (Proverbs 13:22 KJV).

"... *All* these things shall be added unto you" (Matthew 6:33 KJV *emphasis added*)

"'I will shake all nations, and the desired of all nations will come, and I will fill this house with glory', says the LORD Almighty. 'The silver is mine and the gold is mine', declares the LORD Almighty" (Haggai 2:7,8).

"Proclaim further: This what the LORD Almighty says: 'My towns will again overflow with prosperity, and the LORD will again comfort Zion and choose Jerusalem'" (Zechariah 1:17).

"And God is able to make *all* grace abound to you, so that in *all* things at *all* times, having *all* that you need, you will abound in *every good work*... You will be made rich in *every way* so that you can be generous on *every occasion*, and through us your generosity will result in thanksgiving to God" (2 Corinthians 9:8,11 *emphasis added*).

"All the believers were one in heart and mind... *There were no needy persons among them*" (Acts 4:32,34 *emphasis*).

The advance of the gospel to the ends of the earth will require a lot of financial input. This is why God has an end-time plan to transfer the wealth of the world into His Church. Mind you, not everyone will partake of this, but those who seek after the Kingdom of God and His righteousness; those who are ready to channel the wealth towards the purposes of God. Will you be one of them?

As believers break into the realm of financial sufficiency and abundance, the work of God will be aptly funded. The rapidity of the wealth transfer (similar to when Israel plundered the Egyptians - see Exodus 12:35,36) will contribute significantly to the acceleration of God's work. The zeal of the Lord of hosts will bring this to pass.

Insight #10: Strategy of Church planting

"I will build my Church" (Matthew 16:18).

"...with your blood you purchased men for God *from every tribe and language and people and nation.* You have made them to be a kingdom and priests to serve our God, and they will reign on earth" (Revelation 5:9,10 *emphasis added*).

Church planting, it has been argued, is probably the most effective way of fulfilling the Great Commission. In many respects, this is true. The truth is that we *are* expected to plant Churches in every nation as a witness to the rule of Christ in the land and a Banner of His victory. The Churches planted will serve as a centre for reaching others in and around the community. Even though Christ rules over the universe, the extent of His rule is determined by the physical churches planted in every ethnic nation. The local church is the physical expression of Christ's area of domain. It is after "every tribe and language and people and nation" is represented in heaven that we will truly sing, "The kingdom of the world has become the kingdom of our Lord and of his Christ, and he will reign for ever and ever" (Revelation 11:15).

Church planting is an urgent task today. Every existing church should prayerfully consider reproducing another church both home and abroad. Not for the sake of having "x number of branches" in the church organisation, but for the sake of advancing the Kingdom of God. Churches need to *plant* churches. Churches need to *support* Churches (as it was in the days of Paul and Peter - see 1 Corinthians 16:1-4; Romans 15:26). Paul was active in extending Christ's rule because he was a church-planter. As this becomes effective in our time, the work of God will speed up tremendously.

Insight #11: Mobilising Every Available Resource

"Then the LORD said to him, 'What is that in your hand?'" (Exodus 4:2).

"Elisha replied to her, 'How can I help you? Tell me, what do you have in your house?'" (2 Kings 4:2).

"When they had all had enough to eat, he said to his disciples, 'Gather the

pieces that are left over. Let nothing be
wasted'" (John 6:12)

Every available resource is needed for the
completion of the divine mandate. Time, talents,
treasures, money, manpower, methodologies;
everything available must be channelled into the
work of God. Nothing is too small for God to use.
He delights in using small things to do great things.
What is in your hand? What is in your church?
What idea do you have for the advance of the Kingdom? Everything needed is already in our hands.
We only need to look well and maximise their use.
The blessing of God makes all the difference.

Insight #12: The Power of Partnership and Networking

> "I urge you, brothers, by our Lord Jesus
> Christ and by the love of the Spirit, to
> *join me* in my struggle by praying to
> God for me" (Romans 15:10 *emphasis
> added*).

> "And you Philippians yourself will
> know that in the early days of the
> gospel ministry, when I left Macedonia,
> *no church entered into partnership with me
> and opened up [a debit and credit] account
> in giving and receiving except you
> only*" (Philippians 4:15 Amp *emphasis
> added*).

> "When they had done so, they caught such a large number of fish that their nets began to break. *So they signalled to their partners* in the other boat to come and help them, and they came and filled both boats so full that they began to sink" (Luke 5:6,7 *emphasis added*).

> "For we are God's fellow-workers..." (1 Corinthians 3:9).

The end-time mandate of the Church is a mega task. No single Church can fulfil it. No single vision is sufficient. No single man has all the resources needed. God has distributed what it takes for the finishing of the work into different people across the globe. It is not wise at this time to attempt accumulating all the necessary resources by oneself. It is time to network and partner with one another. A Kingdom mentality will ensure this, while anti-kingdom attitudes (like disunity and pride) will hinder it.

In this last hour, one of the most effective ways to accelerate the execution of God's work is networking and partnership - God-ordained partnership. God is linking people with similar visions and kindred spirits together for the advance of the Kingdom. On our own, we are like Ezekiel's dry bones; but as God brings us together by His Spirit, bone to bone, we would rise up a mighty army ready to do battle for the Lord.

If the whole world is linking up in anticipation for the coming of the antichrist, the Church must also unite for the singular pursuit of spreading the glory of God and bringing back our Lord Jesus Christ. It is through unity, Christ said, that the world would know that He is Lord and that we belong to Him (John 17:20-23).

God is linking people with similar visions and kindred spirits together for the advance of the Kingdom.

In every church and para-church ministry, prayer partners are needed. Financial partners are also required. On a ministerial level, preachers and congregations, particularly those in the same city or region, need to network together for the corporate expression of the love of Christ in their area. Each ministry and spiritual gift in the Body should complement one another. The harvest is truly plentiful, but the harvesting partners are few. God send us more godly partners! Give us a networking mentality!

Insight #13: Inspiration, Revelation & Divine Wisdom

> "For the earnest expectation of the creature waiteth for the manifestation of the sons of God" (Romans 8:19 KJV).

> "[God's] intent was that now, through
> the Church, the manifold wisdom of
> God should be made known to the rul-
> ers and authorities in the heavenly
> realms" (Ephesians 3:10).

> "For I will give you words and wisdom
> that none of you adversaries will be able
> to resist and contradict" (Luke 21:15).

> "I keep asking that the God of our Lord
> Jesus Christ, the glorious Father, may
> give you the Spirit of wisdom and
> revelation, so that you may know him
> better" (Ephesians 1:17).

God is up to something in our time! He has a
plan to fully restore His glory in man. He has set
up our generation for the greatest move that the
earth has ever witnessed. The accumulation of
spiritual insight has never been this much. It is
upon this archive of knowledge that the Holy Spirit
will breathe fresh inspiration, which will birth
revelation and a manifestation of divine wisdom.
The combined attack of Satan will prove futile as
the Church, built upon the rock of revelation,
advances in the wisdom of God.

As the Holy Ghost reveals the Word in us, the
Church will mature in revelation knowledge, "until
we all reach unity in the faith *and in the knowledge of
the Son of God* and become mature, attaining unto
the whole measure of the fullness of
Christ" (Ephesians 4:13). If there is anything keep-

ing Christ in heaven apart from the reaching of the nations, it is the maturity of the Church as the above Scripture describes. This shall come to pass in our time through revelation knowledge.

Insight #14: Inward Freedom, Transformation & Deliverance

> "[God] has raised up a horn of salvation for us in the house of his servant David... *to rescue us from the hand of our enemies, and to enable us to serve him* without fear in holiness and righteousness before him all our days" (Luke 1:69, 74,75 *emphasis added*).

> "Then leaving her water jar, the woman went back to the town and said to the people, 'Come, see a man who told me everything I ever did. Could this be the Christ?'. They came out of the town and made their way towards him... Many of the Samaritans from that town believed in him because of the woman's testimony, 'He told me everything I ever did'" (John 4:28,29,39).

> "When they came to see Jesus, they saw the man who had been possessed by the legion of demons sitting there, dressed and in his right mind; and they were afraid... So the man went away and began to tell in the Decapolis (i.e. Ten Cit-

ies) how much Jesus had done for him. And all the people were amazed" (Mark 5:15,20).

"I will *run* in the path of your commands, *for you have set my heart free*." (Psalm 119:32 *emphasis added*).

"Now the Lord is the Spirit, and where the Spirit of the Lord is, *there is freedom*" (2 Corinthians 3:17 *emphasis added*).

The advance of the gospel is in the hands of this generation of believers. However, vast majorities are spiritually bound in one form or the other. Many do not know the reality of complete freedom in Christ. What we need on the harvest field are not just "labourers", but people who are completely emancipated to do the will of God and able to operate victoriously in the realms of the Spirit. There is a task, therefore, to set all the "bound labourers" in the Church free, enabling them to serve the Lord with boldness and holiness. Through "the Spirit of wisdom and revelation", there will be deliverance, because "you will know the truth, and the truth will set you free" (John 8:32).

There is a fresh deposit of revelation in the Church today as to the effects of the past upon the present and future. Many who have lived in the prison of past hurts and pain can experience the freedom in Christ. The Lord is raising more anointed counsellors who know the operation of the gifts of the Spirit and are eager to see people restored into fullness. "Upon mount Zion (the Church) shall be deliverance, and there will be holiness; and the house of Jacob shall possess their possessions" (Obadiah 17 KJV).

> **What we need on the harvest field are not just "labourers", but people who are completely emancipated to do the will of God and able to operate victoriously in the realms of the Spirit.**

The purpose of deliverance and inner transformation, we should keep in mind, is for the accomplishment of the Lord's purposes. The Samaritan woman, after her newfound freedom in Christ, reached a whole community; the healed demoniac reached ten. Inner healing is not an end in itself. It is meant to release the potential of the healed person to do the will of God. Anyone who has been healed must go out and be a vessel of healing for someone else.

Insight #15: Miracles, Signs & Wonders

> "'Unless you people see *miraculous signs and wonders*', Jesus told him, 'you will

never believe'" (John 4:48 *emphasis
added*).

"Then the disciples went out and
preached everywhere, and the Lord
worked with them and confirmed his
word by the *signs* that accompanied
it" (Mark 16:20 *emphasis added*).

"Now Lord, consider their threats and
enable you servants to speak your word
with great boldness. Stretch out your
hand to heal and perform *miraculous
signs and wonders* through the name of
your holy servant Jesus" (Acts 4:29,30
emphasis added).

"When the crowds heard Philip and
saw the *miraculous signs* he did, they all
paid close attention to what he said.
With shrieks, evil spirits came out of
many, and many paralytics and cripples
were healed. *So there was great joy in
that city*" (Acts 8:6-8 *emphasis added*).

The world cannot be reached without the move
of God in miracles, signs and wonders. The ministry of Jesus Christ on earth advanced at a fast rate
because of the constant demonstration of God's
power through Him. The early Church also
reached their known world in the same way
(Hebrews 2:4). If we will reach our world for Jesus,
the miraculous acts of God will feature greatly.
Our God is a God of miracles. Let us present Him

as He is and expect Him to confirm our bold decla-
rations for the sake of His glory.

*****

The baton for the final lap of the divine race is in
our hands. Ours is a generation full of opportunities. We should explore every opening for the
advance of God's Kingdom. This could indeed be
our finest hour. Let us receive revelation from
God's apostles and prophets. Let us learn from
each other. Let us key into the mystery of divine
acceleration and see what God will do through our
obedience. May the pure, undiluted and eternal
word of Christ dwell richly in us at this time. May
there be a strong sense of purpose in the Church
that will keep us in the will of God. Like David,
may we not sleep until God's purpose for this
generation is fully accomplished.

> "For when David had served God's
> purpose in his own generation, he fell
> asleep; he was buried with his fathers
> and his body decayed" (Acts 13:36).

9 | THE SPIRIT AND THE BRIDE

The seconds on the clock of history seem to tick away faster than ever. The purposes of God are about to end. There can be no more delay until the Lord appears in His glory. According to prophecy and the signs of the time, Christ's second coming is imminent.

A MATTER OF EMPHASIS

We all know the seriousness of Christ's departing words to the Church, the commission He gave us before ascending into heaven. These words cannot be taken lightly. The subject matter was the main issue on His mind before He left the disciples.

The words of a dying man are very important. Even though Christ, before His ascension, was not "dying", He still had some last instructions for the Church. "Over a period of forty days," the Bible says that, "[He] spoke [to the disciples] about the kingdom of God" (Acts 1:3b). He also restated, in clear words, the mandate He was leaving for them to carry out. We have the privilege of reading this mandate in the four gospels and the book of Acts (Matthew 28:18,19; Mark 16:15,16; Luke 24:46-48; John 20:21 & Acts 1:8).

There is a reason why there are *five* records of this command and why Christ repeated it before He left the earth. There is a reason why the Great Commission was the last words on His lips as He was ascending into heaven. The reason is for the sake of emphasis.

This could, in fact, be stated as a principle underscoring God's pronouncements:

> Whenever God makes a statement more than once, he does so for the sake of emphasising its importance and infallibility.

By repeating a statement, God is establishing an eternal oracle, the weight of His Person being an oath for its fulfilment. If it is a command, He wants the recipients of the command to take it as seriously as He does. If it is a promise, He wants the recipients to believe that it will come to pass no matter the circumstances.

It is a dangerous thing to under-emphasise the things that God has put an emphasis upon. Christ's last words fall into this category of emphasised statements.

When God speaks once, we hear twice. When He speaks twice, the matter is inscribed on tablets of stone as an eternal witness. When He speaks more than twice, no human vocabulary can describe the seriousness God attaches to the word. Heaven and earth (and God Himself) will have to pass away for such a word to go unfulfilled.

> "Every matter must be *established* by the testimony of two or three witnesses" (2 Corinthians 13:1 *emphasis added*)

> "The reason the dream was given to Pharaoh in *two forms* is that *the matter has been firmly decided by God, and God will do it soon*" (Genesis 41:32 *emphasis added*).

Why have I written all this? First, to make us realise the importance of the Great Commission, the departing words Christ uttered repeatedly after His earthly ministry. But also, to reveal the seriousness in another *last* statement of Christ.

CHRIST'S VERY "LAST" WORDS

The concluding book of the Bible, the book of Revelation, is of great importance. Jesus Christ, as it were, "dictated" the contents of the book to His

servant John. He also made clear how He wants us
to respond to the revelations it contains:

> "Blessed is the one who *reads* the words
> of this prophecy, and blessed are those
> who *hear* it and *take to heart* what is
> written in it, because the time is
> near" (Revelation 1:3; see also
> 22:6,7,10,18,19 *emphasis added*).

Many times in this book, Jesus said, "He who
was an ear, let him hear what the Spirit says to the
Churches" (Revelation 2:7,11,17,29; 3:6,13,22).

**It is a dangerous thing
to under-emphasise the
things that God has put an
emphasis upon.**

Now, if the last book in God's Book is of great
importance, then the *last* chapter of this *last* book
must be of double importance. Every verse needs
close scrutiny and careful attention.

In this last chapter of God's only Book to man,
we have Christ's last words. No doubt, everything
He said in this last chapter is significant. However,
recalling the principle of repetition and emphasis, a
particular statement of Christ demands our whole
attention because He uttered it not once, not twice,
but three times:

"Behold, I am coming soon!" (Revelation 22:7).

"Behold, I am coming soon!" (Revelation 22:12).

"Yes, I am coming soon" (Revelation 22:20).

Remember: When God speaks once, we hear twice; when He speaks twice, the words are inscribed on tablets of stone as an eternal witness; when he speaks more than twice, no human vocabulary can describe God's commitment to bringing the word to pass. Heaven and earth (and even God Himself) will have to pass away for the word to go unfulfilled.

"I AM COMING SOON!"

Jesus Christ is coming soon!

Jesus Christ is coming soon!

Jesus Christ is coming soon!

Jesus Christ is coming soon!

Jesus Christ is coming soon!

Jesus Christ is coming soon!

Jesus Christ is coming soon!

Writing this statement a million times is not enough to convey its weightiness. It is a reality that will come to pass before this age draws to a close. It is a fact that will soon manifest. Jesus Christ is coming soon! The foolishness of mockers cannot annul the eventuality of Christ's appearance (2 Peter 3:3-10).

Jesus Christ is coming soon! His coming will be the climax of God's purpose for the Church age. It will come to pass at the fullness of time. Purpose necessitated the first advent of Christ. Purpose will again bring Him to earth. The angels were right when they proclaimed *"This same Jesus*, who has been taken from you into heaven, *will come back* in the same way you have seen him go into heaven" (Acts 1:11 *emphasis added*).

Jesus Christ is coming soon! Writing this statement a million times is not enough to convey its weightiness.

It is one thing to know that Christ is coming, and another thing to hear the sound in the Spirit that He is actually, as it were, on His way. The ten virgins were prompted to trim their lamps because they *heard* the sound of the bridegroom's arrival (Matthew 25:1-13). Elijah heard the sound of rain before it physically poured on the earth.

End-time rain is about to pour. Now is the time to prepare.

The Bridegroom is on His way. Now is the time to get ready for Him.

The signs of the time are clear. The events of the age are revealing. Let Him that has an ear, hear what the Spirit is saying to the Church.

REFOCUSING ON PURPOSE

Now, when Christ was leaving the earth, the disciples were faced with a temptation that many people have fallen into over the years. They wanted to know the specific date of Christ's second coming and the time of Israel's restoration.

> "'Tell us', they said, *'When will all this happen,* and what will be sign of your coming and of the end of the age?'" (Matthew 24:3 *emphasis added*).

> "So when they met together, they asked him, 'Lord, are you *at this time* going to restore the kingdom of Israel?'" (Acts 1:6 *emphasis added*).

Many preachers and students of the Bible, as they read the book of Revelation (and other prophetic books), have fallen into the trap of date-setting and date-suggesting. This inquisitiveness is nothing but a subtle distraction from purpose. Christ's reply to the disciples' question on timing was meant to refocus their attention on the mandate they had already received:

> "He said to them: 'It is not for you to know the times or dates the Father has set by his own authority. *But* you will

receive power when the Holy Spirit comes on you; and you will be my witnesses in Jerusalem, and in all Judea and Samaria, and to the ends of the earth" (Acts 1:7,8 *emphasis added*).

In other words, Christ was telling His disciples not to bother about the exact dates of His return, but instead to get down to Kingdom business immediately the Holy Spirit comes upon them.

In the same manner, "I am coming soon" for us means "I am coming soon" and nothing more. We are not to take the book of Revelation (or any other book of the Bible) and search out the dates of Christ's coming. Instead, we should focus on the completion of the unfinished work now that the Holy Spirit has come upon us!

KINGDOM PARTNERSHIP

There is no way we can complete this assignment without the partnership of the Holy Spirit. The disciples were forbidden to do anything or go anywhere until the promised Holy Spirit came upon them. After the Holy Spirit came, the once timid disciples became bold witnesses of the resurrection of Jesus. The Lord confirmed their bold words with signs and wonders. The gospel spread rapidly as the Church committed herself to partnership with the Holy Spirit.

The Spirit is already here - for a purpose. The final chapter of God's Book clearly reveals this purpose. Once again, this is done for emphasis:

> *"The Spirit and the bride say, 'Come!'* And let him who hears say, 'Come!' Whoever is thirsty, let him come; and whoever wishes, let him take the free gift of the water of life" (Revelation 22:17 *emphasis added*).

"The Spirit and the bride". This is end-time Kingdom partnership. The Spirit is here for God's business, but He needs our total co-operation for a successful enterprise. If we must finish the work of God, we necessarily have to acknowledge, appreciate and appropriate the divine partnership of the Spirit. The Spirit is focused. He cannot be distracted into any other business other than the business of proclaiming "Come!" This should be our business too if we are really in tune with Him.

As we partner with God in the execution of His purpose (the restoration of all things and missionary outreach to all the nations of the world), the Spirit will accomplish through us great things that we cannot do by ourselves. Signs and wonders will authenticate the words we preach. The wealth of the wicked will transfer to us for the sole purpose of financing God's business. Heaven will stand at attention as we intercede for the nations in the strength of the Holy Ghost. The will of God will be done and His Kingdom will come as the Spirit leads us into all the earth. This is true Kingdom partnership - active involvement in the work of God with the help of the Holy Spirit.

THE REWARDS OF KINGDOM PARTNERSHIP

God will reward everyone who partners with Him in this end-time enterprise.

> "Behold, I am coming soon! *My reward is with me, and I will give to everyone according to what he has done*" (Revelation 22:12 *emphasis added*).

> "The man who plants and the man who waters have one purpose, *and each will be rewarded according to his own labour. For we are God's fellow-workers; you are God's field, God's building*" (1 Corinthians 3:8,9 *emphasis added*).

Since the beginning of time, God has called men to be fellow-workers (partners) with Him. God called Abraham, Moses, David and the long list of faith-heroes with the promise of both eternal and earthly reward.

The Spirit is here for God's business, but He needs our total co-operation for a successful enterprise.

This call is coming to *you* today. Will you partner with God? Will you involve yourself with His work? Will you do whatever *He* requires of you? As we have seen, areas of involvement are diverse today. There cannot be any excuse for non-involvement.

If we attempt to broadly classify our participation in kingdom activity under three headings, these will be the categories (commonly used by churches and missions organisations):

Praying

Will you devote yourself to praying "Kingdom of God, come; will of God, be done"?

Will you pray for total restoration in the Church?

Will you pray for missionaries on the field?

Will you pray for leaders in the Church?

Will you sign up to pray for the 10/40 and 40/70 window nations?

Will you pray for the glory of God to fill the earth as the waters cover the sea?

Will you allow the Holy Spirit to pray *in* and *through* you the will of God?

Giving

Will you give towards world evangelisation?

Will you support missionaries on the field?

Will you determine to be a faithful steward of the finances God entrusts into your hand?

Will you support corporate programmes that will impact and influence the Church?

Will you give towards the work of your local assembly?

Will you give what you can so that someone can hear the good news?

Will you help to make resources available to workers on the field?

Going

Will you be a witness for Christ wherever you find yourself?

Will you consider going on a short-term mission outreach?

Will you go wherever the Lord sends you?

Will you do whatever the Lord asks you to do?

Will you say whatever the Lord asks you to say?

Will you go into the nations of the earth?

Will you be actively involved in God's end-time business?

Even though Kingdom Partnership may require an abandonment of self and worldly pleasure, the investment is worthwhile. We have the promise of a hundred-fold return in this life and in the life to come.

> "Jesus said to them, 'I tell you the truth,
> at the renewal of all things, when the
> Son of Man sits on his glorious throne,
> you who have followed me will also sit
> on twelve thrones, judging the twelve

tribes of Israel. And everyone who has left houses or brothers or sisters or father or mother or children or fields for my sake *will receive a hundred times as much and will inherit eternal life"* (Matthew 19:28,29 *emphasis added*).

It is time to get down to business. It is time for the Church to be one. It is time for every nation, tribe and tongue to witness the glory of God. Jesus must be enthroned as Lord over the nations. His enemies must be subdued under His feet. We must make it happen because this is why we are here.

Even though Kingdom Partnership may require an abandonment of self and worldly pleasure, the investment is worthwhile.

"AMEN. COME, LORD JESUS"

Christ's proclamation, "I am coming soon", will not materialise until it is seconded by the Church. Even though He made this promise more than 2,000 years ago, He is yet to come. The generation of believers that truly says "Amen" to His coming will be the one to witness the long-awaited appearance of the Lord of glory.

The "Amen" we need to say is not just in words, but in purposeful activity. For so long, the Church has not joined the chorus that expresses the desire for the Lord's coming. Sections of the Church may be busy here and there, but it will take the entire Church to cry out for the coming of the Lord. We all need to agree in our hearts for the Lord to come, and show forth our agreement by our actions. We need to "go on to maturity" (Hebrews 6:1) and get busy with establishing God's rule all over the earth.

There is a cry coming back to the Church of our generation. The cry will bring back our Lord and Saviour. It is an eleventh-hour-cry that we must utter until it is heeded. Church, let us in unity cry out, "Maranatha, Come Lord Jesus!" This is our preordained destiny. Nothing else that we may desire can compare with His manifest, physical presence. This is where God has been leading us. This is where the Spirit is urging us to speedily run. This is the finish line before us. This is why you have read this book to the very last page. Let us not stop crying until God hears us from heaven above: *"Amen. Come, Lord Jesus"* (Revelation 22:20).

> "The grace of the Lord Jesus be with God's people. Amen" (Revelation 22:21).

APPENDICES

APPENDIX A: QUESTIONS TO SELAH® UPON

CHAPTER ONE:
REDISCOVERING THE GOD OF PURPOSE

1. How can an understanding of God's purpose affect your involvement in God's kingdom?

2. Regarding God's agenda for this age of grace, what is the importance for us in knowing where we are currently positioned - at *beginning* or *ending* of the age?

3. How does the statements "I have finished my course" (Paul) and "I came to... finish His work" (Christ) affect how you commit yourself to God's mandate for your life?

4. Recalling the picture of a relay race, what is the agenda of the Holy Spirit in the world today and how do you fit into the picture?

CHAPTER TWO:
ADVANCING THE KINGDOM BY FORCE (I)

1. What part do we have to play in the advancement and fulfilment of God's prophecies?

2. Why is it important for God to find people who will run with all that is in His heart and mind?

3. What effect could an encounter with God's heartbeat have upon your life?

4. In what ways have you felt the strong hand of the Lord intervening in your circumstances to conform you to His will for your life?

5. While tragedies like accidents and death are not the doing of the Lord, is there any reason to believe God can allow affliction to break our resistance of His will?

CHAPTER THREE:
ADVANCING THE KINGDOM BY FORCE (II)

1. In what ways are traditions and practices in the Church hindering the advancement of God's kingdom today?

2. Can you identify in your own life recent instructions from God that demand activity beyond your comfort zones?

3. What are some of the changes that are imperative before there could be an advancement of God's purpose in your life and in the Church?

4.   What role does praying in accordance to God's will play in moving the things of God forward in the earth?

CHAPTER FOUR:
WHY IS CHRIST STILL SITTING IN HEAVEN?

1.   What are the lessons you can learn from Christ's passion to do the will of the Father?

2.   For how long did the Father indicate that Christ will have to sit at His right hand in heaven?

3.   As the Body of Christ, how does our exercise of Kingdom authority upon the earth affect the timing of Christ's return?

4.   What are the *kairos* conditions that must be fulfilled before Christ returns for His Church?

5.   What are the two streams of *kairos* conditions and how involved are you in each of them?

CHAPTER FIVE:
THE GREAT TRANSITION

1.   What is the place of willingness in advancing the purposes of God in these last days?

2.   How does revival transform in the heart of God's people toward His work?

3.   How desirous are you for a move of God in your life?

4.   How should we respond to the revelation of God's word today?

5.   What is the link between joy in heaven and the willingness of God's people to work the works of God?

CHAPTER SIX:
THE NIGHT IS PREGNANT?

1.   How does wilderness seasons of life prepare people to do the will of God?

2.   Can you identify people and situations that God has been preparing you to minister into based on the affliction you have endured in recent times?

3.   What is the role of "youthfulness" in the kingdom today?

4.   How can the "young" and "old" join hands together to run the final race of destiny?

5.   As a leader, what steps are you taking to raise and release other ministries according to Ephesians 4:11-14?

6.   How can we prioritise holiness in the same way that God does?

CHAPTER SEVEN:
HOW FAR CAN YOU SEE?

1.   How did God demonstrate the wisdom of vision in the execution of His redemption plan

and why was it impossible for Satan to decode God's plan?

2. How did Paul's vision to reach the Gentiles complement Peter's vision to reach the Jews?

3. What role does love for God and love for the brethren play in uniting the Church in the purpose of God?

4. How are you contributing to restoration in the Church and/or the reaching of all nations? How is your congregation contributing?

5. What is your personal vision statement? What is the vision statement of your church? Is it written?

CHAPTER EIGHT: THE MYSTERY OF DIVINE ACCELERATION

1. How does our changing world and the seemingly speeding up of time affect your conduct and attitude in the kingdom of God?

2. How does "Rounding-Up" describe our time more accurately than "Revival" or "Restoration"?

3. How does the Spirit and the Word of God launch us into the mainstream of God's agenda?

4. How can you keep in step with God in the fast and changing world?

5. Going through the insights for divine acceleration, in which areas do you need a mentality

change to be in tune with what God is doing in these last days?

6.   Which portion of Scripture has significantly influenced your thinking in recent times?

CHAPTER NINE:
THE SPIRIT AND THE BRIDE

1.   Why did Christ repeat "the Great Commission" before ascending into heaven and why do we have five records of the commission in the New Testament?

2.   What is the relevance of the last book of the Bible and the last chapter of this last book?

3.   The imminent return of Christ to the earth was reiterated thrice in the last chapter of God's book. What should this mean to the Church?

4.   How did Jesus refocus the attention of His disciples when they asked Him about the exact timing of His coming?

5.   How can we best join hands with the Holy Spirit to fulfil the singular agenda for which He is in the world?

6.   What kind of rewards are awaiting those who walk and work with God?

7.   Can you make a list of the opportunities you have to be a part of what God is doing in the world today?

8.   Have you prayed lately, "Come, Lord Jesus"?

APPENDIX B: SUGGESTED READING

Barna, George. *The Power of Vision*, Ventura, CA, Regal Books, 1992.

Barna, George. *Turning Vision Into Action*, Ventura, CA, Regal Books, 1996.

Bonnke, Reinhard. *Evangelism by Fire*, Eastbourne, East Sussex, Kingsway Publications, 1989.

Cunningham, Loren. *Is That Really You, God?* Seattle, WA, YWAM Publishing, 1984.

Duewel, Wesley. *Touch the World Through Prayer*, Grand Rapids, Michigan, Zondervan Publishing House, 1986.

Emmanuel, Tokunbo. *Rediscovering God*, London, UK, Emmanuel House, 1993.

Emmanuel, Tokunbo. *The Charismatic Agenda*, London, UK, Emmanuel House, 2000.

Emmanuel, Tokunbo. *Ultimate Destiny*, London, UK, Generation Z, 2001.

Johnstone, Patrick &. Mandryk, Jason *Operation World*, Waynesboro, GA, Paternoster, 2002.

Hamon, Bill. *The Day of the Saints*, Shippensburg, PA, Destiny Image Publishers, 2002.

McClung, Floyd; Blessitt, Arthur et al. *The Final Frontier*, Eastbourne, East Sussex, Kingsway Publications, 1987.

Mitchell, Roger & Sue. *Target Europe*, Tonbridge, England, Sovereign World, 2001.

Olonade, Timothy. *Battle Cry for the Nations*, Jos, Nigeria, CAPRO Media, 1995.

Pirolo, Neal. *Serving as Senders*, San Diego, Califonia, Emmaus Road International, 1991.

Shibley, David. *Once in a Lifetime*, Tonbridge, England, Sovereign World, 1997

Sjogren, Bob & Stearns, Bill & Amy. *Run With the Vision*, Minneapolis, Minnesota, Bethany House Publishers, 1995.

Stearns, Bill & Amy. *Catch the Vision 2000*, Minneapolis, Minnesota, Bethany House Publishers, 1991.

Verwer, George. *Out of the Comfort Zone*, Waynesboro, GA, OM Paternoster, 2000.

OTHER BOOKS BY TOKUNBO EMMANUEL

Rediscovering God (96-page paperback)

Since the expulsion of man from Eden, God has continued to reveal Himself to those who express a hunger for Him. Our generation not only has the privilege of accumulated knowledge but also the inspiration of the Holy Spirit. Rediscovering the fullness of God's Word through the activity of the Spirit is a unique feature of the final revival that the end-time Church will experience.

ISBN 1-900529-05-X (£4.99)

The Charismatic Agenda (96–paged paperback)

*In this apologetic, the question is asked: **What in the world are we up to?** An exposition on Christ's words, "Not everyone who says to me 'Lord, Lord' will enter the kingdom of heaven, but only he who does the will of my Father who is in heaven." (Matthew 7:21). A "must" read before standing before the judgement seat of Christ.*

ISBN 1-900529-10-6 (£4.99)

Ultimate Destiny (160–paged paperback)

A major prophetic work that clearly reveals the Holy Spirit's "unity agenda" in the Church. We cannot really enjoy God's best until we all unite together to celebrate the Kingship of Jesus Christ. Although already a reality "in Him", it is important that we express our oneness at the Lord's table and in our daily relationships. This is our ultimate destiny as the Body of Christ on earth.

ISBN 1-900529-20-3 (£5.99)

The Selah Verses (64–paged paperback)

You can now read and meditate on all the verses in the Psalms that have the "Selah" punctuation. These seventy-four verses (including three in Habakkuk) touch on a variety of issues and open the reader to heavenly inspiration. With an introduction explaining the meaning of Selah and five articles to Selah® upon, you will certainly be enriched in your heart.

ISBN 1-900529-27-0 (£2.99)

Other titles out of print:

- *Revival in the Desert*
- *Sharing the Word of God*
- *The Glory of Young Men*
- *31 Nuggets of Inspiration*

Titles available at bookshops:
Or
Email: sales@bwam.org
Visit: www.bwam.org

INTRODUCING BOOKS WITH A MISSION (BWAM)

Books With A Mission (BWAM) is a publishing and missions movement established for spreading the knowledge of God's glory to the ends of the earth. Through the production and global distribution of books and relevant spiritual resources, a difference is being made in the nations.

BWAM activities include:

- Opening resource centres for believers in nations around the world

- Supplying books to missionaries, Bible School libraries, colleges etc.

- Developing and supporting relevant indigenous publishing programmes in different nations.

- Raising funds for missions and missionaries through the global marketing and sales of best-selling books.

*For more information about BWAM,
BWAM Projects, Donate-A-Book weeks
or for a catalogue of products, visit:
www.bwam.org*

IF THIS BOOK HAS BEEN A BLESSING TO YOU,
PLEASE WRITE TO:
COMMENTS@BWAM.ORG
OR
BWAM
PO BOX 15022
LONDON
SE5 7ZL
UNITED KINGDOM

The *Mega! Books* mandate:

To publish works for Kingdom advance;

books that are

Prophetic

Provoking

Definitive

&

Relevant.

"The Lion has roared - who will not fear?
The Sovereign Lord has spoken - who can but prophesy?"
(Amos 3:8).